Claude Duval has been racing correspondent for *The Sun* since 1967. Apart from flat and steeplechase racing, Duval's chief interests are cricket and golf.

'Written in a racy style which takes the reader along at a rare pace'
Peter Willet, *Sporting Chronicle*

'Duval does a very good job, giving a real insight into the life of Lester Piggott and just what makes him tick'
John Forbes, *Manchester Evening News*

'Here's a book that makes you really know Piggott's genius'
The Sun

'A very readable insight into Lester Piggott's achievements and rare lifestyle'
Peter Scott, *Daily Telegraph*

By the same author

Pat on the Back
Willie Carson's Story
Minter – The Autobiography

CLAUDE DUVAL

Lester

PANTHER
Granada Publishing

Granada Publishing Limited
8 Grafton Street,
London W1X 3LA

Published by Panther Books 1979

Revised edition published 1985

First published in Great Britain by
Stanley Paul & Co Ltd 1972

Copyright © Claude Duval 1972, 1979

ISBN 0–586–06874–0

Printed and bound in Great Britain by
Anchor Brendon Ltd, Tiptree, Essex

Set in Times

Contents

CHAPTER ONE

King of the Classics

God threw away the mould when Lester Piggott was born on Guy Fawkes' day in 1935. No single man has ever made such a tremendous impact on the world of horse racing since the faraway days of the Stuart monarchs when they changed the unknown village of Newmarket into the centre of the sport. Lester has become a legend in his own lifetime – arguably the most famous Englishman living – and his name known throughout the world. The poker-faced pilot with the touch of a genius has won the reputation of being the greatest jockey of all time. From Newmarket to New Zealand, from Ascot to Arlington Park, his deeds in the saddle are legendary. His lined face – likened to a well-kept grave – bears witness to his never-ending wasting and constant battle with the scales. When he retired from the saddle at the end of the 1985 season, a legend folded. Only Fred Archer, Steve Donoghue and Sir Gordon Richards can come anywhere near Piggott's greatness. He's a world figure, better known than the Prime Minister and certainly a bigger wage earner.

Yet, paradoxically, Lester's a loner. He is totally solitary and withdrawn, partly because of his deafness and speech impediment. Millions love to watch his power-packed finishes but he still remains an unknown character even to his closest friends. His professional partnerships with Sir Noel Murless, Vincent O'Brien, Robert Sangster, Henry Cecil and Daniel Wildenstein all had their tense moments. Ironically, Lester ended his career as a freelance. A loner.

Only Sir Gordon Richards with 4,870 wins has ridden

more winners than Lester's total of 4,307 at the start of 1985. But Piggott has ridden more than 300 winners in France and his overall world total would take him way past Sir Gordon. There's hardly a racing country in the world where he has not returned to his favourite spot . . . the winner's enclosure.

But it's in the Classics, the ultimate test for horse and rider, that Piggott has galloped into an unassailable lead over his rivals. He has courted controversy and been involved in blazing rows all his life. But nobody could ever question that given the best horse for a big race, his success rate is uncanny. His brilliant record of 29 Classic wins will surely never be beaten. His record of nine Derby victories puts him up on a pedestal way above his rivals. Fred Archer, who ended up shooting himself not a furlong from Lester's Newmarket home at 29 because of wasting problems, had 21 Classic wins. In recent years Piggott has made the Classics his very own super show.

A measure of Piggott's flair for the big occasion can be seen in his last seven Classic wins – FIVE were gained in photo-finishes, four by a neck, and one by a short head. He's made millions for his lucky owners by the length of just a few nostrils.

It would be easy to put down Piggott's craving for cash as the prime reason for his success, but that would be unkind and untrue. His famous love of 'readies' has driven him to extremes but his bank of experience going back to 1948 has always enabled him to outwit his opponents. A fine judge of pace, combined with tremendous power, has made him unbeatable. Casting one's mind back to find when he has ridden a bad race is a hard job.

Admired, almost hero worshipped . . . and yet to some extent unloved. This is the paradox of Piggott. Perhaps people recognize his tremendously ruthless streak and find it a little hard to swallow. Others find that the way he has 'jocked off' so many other jockeys over the years not the act of the greatest sportsman. Others wince at the way his machine-gun tactics with his famous wand often lifts horses over the line. But virtually all the controversial 'jockeying off' incidents have ended with the classic question – would any other jockey but Piggott and his powerful tactics have won the race? The answer is virtually always 'No'.

Many times I have expected to see horses coming back with as many stripes as *The Times* crossword, but there hasn't been a mark on them. Piggott's greatness is defined in the two extremes. He can biff, bang, wallop one home, but at the other end of the spectrum he can deliver a horse to win as a thing of beauty. It's a very rare talent. His 1957 Oaks win on The Queen's Carrozza was one of his best-ever rides, but the filly probably didn't think so. She had to be beaten like a carpet to land the Classic. Sir Ivor and Nijinsky were totally different displays – late runs timed to the split second.

But I think Piggott's eighth Derby win on The Minstrel convinced me that if there has ever been a greater jockey I haven't heard of him. No other man who ever swung his leg over a horse would have won on The Minstrel. Again Piggott knew the form-book backwards. He had ridden the runner-up Hot Grove to win the Chester Vase and he also knew all about the favourite Blushing Groom. Quipped Lester, 'Funny old game, isn't it? I could have ridden any of the first three. I simply wore 'em all down.'

Piggott has been known to get it wrong. He thought that Wollow was a certainty for the 1976 Derby. Wollow was unbeaten in six races and had already won the 2,000 Guineas in fine style. Now at 11–10 he was the red-hot favourite . . . and turned out to be the shortest priced Derby losing favourite since Tudor Minstrel in 1947. 'It will take a gun to stop Wollow winning', forecast Piggott in his ghosted column in the *Evening Standard*. He didn't give a hope to Empery, who had lost both his two previous races. He was trained in France by colourful Maurice Zilber, who once boasted 'I can walk on water'. Indian-born Zilber wasn't too happy to learn of Piggott's Wollow forecast. He phoned Lester on the eve of the Derby and said, 'A gun! You wouldn't need a gun to stop Wollow. You have the great Maurice . . . and Empery!'

If Piggott had dedicated his life to being a roulette player he still would have ended up being a multi-millionaire. He nearly always picks the right number, or the right selection, when the wheel of fate spins for a big race. This was never better shown than before the 1975 Oaks when Lester used all his cunning and judgement to enable him to equal Fred Archer's total of 21 Classic winners.

Jeremy Tree decided to run both Juliette Marny and Brilliantine in the Oaks. Because of the going he left his decision until lunchtime of the day of the race. He recalls, 'I told Lester that as I was running both fillies he would have to decide which one he wanted to be on. He shrugged his shoulders and said, "No. I think you ought to decide." I said I honestly wasn't keen to nominate one or the other. I insisted that Piggott made the choice. He paused for a few seconds and then said, "I'll ride Juliette Marny."' Wearing blinkers for the first time she won in a canter . . . Brilliantine finished last but one. Punters did not realize the jockey situation and she was allowed to drift out from 8–1 to 12–1. It was a classic example of the need for overnight declaration of jockeys. Juliette Marny and Piggott went on to win the Irish Oaks by a neck.

Perhaps Piggott's worst Classic ride was on Rose Bowl, the 7–4 favourite for the 1975 1,000 Guineas. Piggott seemed to have her in all the wrong positions. She was terribly baulked and when she eventually saw daylight she finished like a train to be fourth behind Nocturnal Spree.

Piggott has diced with death several times in his career. If you spend over thirty years steering tons of horseflesh at breakneck speeds it is bound to be so. In the 1977 Oaks he was on the warm favourite, Durtal. As she went out on to the course she took fright, the saddle slipped and Piggott, with one foot still in the iron, was dragged along for forty yards until the filly crashed into a concrete post. Piggott was very dazed but lucky that his foot came loose just before

10

Durtal collided. The horse was obviously withdrawn but Piggott showed his courage one hour later when he won on Elland Road for his brother-in-law Robert Armstrong.

Over the years Piggott has had many clashes with the stewards. But he has only suffered one lengthy ban for being on a 'non trier'. In 1962 at the old Lincoln course Piggott rode Ione in a seller for Bob Ward, who also trained another horse in the race, Polly Macaw, ridden by the late Peter Robinson. Polly Macaw was backed down to evens favourite with Ione going out to 11–8. Polly Macaw duly beat the stable companion by two lengths. After an extended inquiry the stewards stood Piggott down from 4 June to 28 July. Ward was found to have been party to the race result and had his trainer's licence withdrawn totally, although he did get it back later.

In 1979 came the famous whip-borrowing incident in the Grand Prix de Deauville. Piggott had the cheek to snatch the whip from Alain Lequeux after he had dropped his own. Piggott went on to finish second on African Hope and duly handed back Lequeux's whip after the finishing line. Unfortunately for Piggott the stewards spotted his little borrowing act and gave him a 21-day suspension. This meant that Piggott missed riding in the St Leger and luckless Lequeux had the last laugh by winning the Classic on Son of Love. The actual whip was later auctioned by Peter O'Sullevan at a stable lads' boxing evening in London.

Over the years Piggott has had no firmer admirer than O'Sullevan, who has the Mike Yarwood ability to do a very fair impersonation of Lester's monosyllabic mutterings. I asked O'Sullevan to recall the one race of Piggott's career which stands out in his mind among the countless he had broadcast. Said O'Sullevan, 'There are so many. Most people would go for the obvious one like Roberto winning the Derby. Nobody else would have won on him that day. But I would go to the other end of the spectrum and select his handling of the 1984 Oaks winner Circus Plume. It's worth watching a video of that race a hundred times.

People are apt to recall the biff, bang, wallop displays but this showed the other side of Lester's immense talent. He had the coolness to appreciate that there was only one way she would win. He sat quietly on her and didn't even breathe down her back. It was the complete display of horsemanship and she probably didn't even know that she had been in a race. A few days later I saw Piggott and said, 'You gave that filly a brilliant ride, didn't you?' Piggott just replied, "She's a little bit funny, you know."'

Several trainers over the years have slammed the 'Long Fella' for his tactics. 'Move over, grandad, I'm coming through' is the much-quoted remark he is claimed to have made to Sir Gordon Richards at Ascot in the 'fifties. It's been denied so many times it must be true. Top Irish trainer Paddy Prendergast once stormed, 'I wouldn't employ Piggott again for all the Crown Jewels', but of course he did so within a matter of weeks. Bill O'Gorman, the talented but outspoken Newmarket trainer, swore, 'He'll never ride for me again', after Piggott finished fourth on Abdu in the Champagne Stakes. French owner Daniel Wildenstein joined the 'Piggott will never ride for me again' club which cost Piggott a winning Arc ride on All Along. Wildenstein has changed his mind many times over jockeys and trainers, but he kept his word over Piggott and refused to let Lester don the famous blue silks ever again.

But the best tale on this theme came at Kempton in 1976. The Honourable Ben Leigh, son of Lord Leigh, took out a trainer's licence for just five years. Fun-loving Ben recalls, 'Piggott rode a filly for me called Nigaire. It was just before the Derby and Piggott was obviously looking after himself. The saddle came off in the parade ring and the horse trod on it. Lester was not keen to get on her and eventually persuaded the stewards that the filly was unsound and got her withdrawn. I was absolutely furious'.

Leigh, even smaller than Piggott, dashed after the world's greatest jockey and, wagging his finger furiously in his face, bellowed, 'You little twat. You will never ride for me again.' Without blinking an eyelid Piggott replied, 'In that case I suppose I'd better pack the game in.'

Thankfully Piggott did not retire on the spot and race-goers for many more years were able to wonder at the greatest horseman ever to go riding by.

CHAPTER TWO

Wantage finds another 'Great'

Perhaps Wantage, the small town in the Vale of the White Horse and at the foot of the rambling Berkshire Downs, was picked out specially by history as the birthplace of the 'greats'. For Alfred the Great, hailed by historians as the finest ruler of England, was born in Wantage. And so, too, was the jockey who, years later, was to carve his name so deeply into the history of the Turf that even the immortal names of Gordon Richards, Steve Donoghue and Fred Archer become almost also-rans compared with the magical name of Lester Piggott.

Gaze at the statue of Alfred the Great overlooking the picturesque market place and it's hard to imagine what the surroundings must have been like when he was born in A.D. 848. Since then the world has stayed the same shape. But that's just about where the similarity ends. Progress has powered on relentlessly, and it's worth noting that the first steam tramway in England linked Wantage with Wantage Road in 1873.

Yes, we know what's happened since the days of King Alfred and how the night of November 5th, 1935, was to be the start of a racing legend which will never be equalled again.

Youngsters who love cricket always regret that they never saw W. G. Grace standing in lordly fashion at the crease before sending a ball crashing to the boundary as the hansom cabs travelled by.

Fight fans curse the fact that they never saw Jack Dempsey, Joe Louis or Rocky Marciano in their prime. How

14

would these giants of the ring have compared with modern-day legend Muhammad Ali?

As far as racing is concerned we are lucky. Perhaps we live with the threat of the world being wiped out in one split-second bombardment, but at least racing fans are lucky to live in the knowledge that usually when they switch on their television sets or go to the racecourses of Britain and France they are watching the greatest jockey who ever climbed on to the back of horseflesh.

Wantage produced Alfred the Great and also Piggott the Great.

Horses moved uneasily in the racing stables of Wantage those years ago when Piggott was born. It was the one night of the year they really hated . . . Guy Fawkes Night.

Like all animals they live in nothing but fear as the fireworks explode. In their minds they must think that the world has gone crazy. It's a nervous experience for the un-lucky animals, but for racing this particular Guy Fawkes Night was to be the start of something which was later really going to explode on the scene with a terrific bang.

Yet perhaps it was all so predictable, nearly as obvious as a straight forecast in a two-horse race.

Watching Piggott strolling out of the weighing room at any racecourse any day you'll probably first notice the thin-ness of the 5 ft 7½ in. frame. He's been called racing's walk-ing skeleton who never gets boxed in.

As he strolls out to the paddock tapping his whip against his right leg, it's hard to imagine that his legend probably started way back in the late 1700's with a loud, jolly man who weighed more than 20 stone.

But this is where the legend of Lester Piggott kicked off.

The gentleman's name was John Day. He trained at Mere just a little over a hundred years after Charles had gone to the George in 1651 in disguise after the Battle of Worcester.

Now racegoers probably know the Wiltshire town as the nearest spot before the charming little National Hunt track of Wincanton, which is a pleasant, largely farmers' meeting.

John Day I was a farmer as well as a pretty shrewd

trainer. He had quite a bit of success before he switched his training headquarters to Houghton Down in Hampshire.

He had several sons and one of them, Sam, was to become a jockey. The Lester Piggott legend was well under way.

Sam was a fine horseman and it came as no surprise to his family when he won the Derby three times. His first triumph was on Gustavus in 1821. Nine years later he was back in the Derby winner's enclosure after riding Priam to victory. In 1846 he steered home Pyrrhus the First.

Another of John Day I's sons became a vet and so continued the family's interest in horses. Charles wasn't so keen on the way of life and emigrated to Russia.

Perhaps it was John Day II, another son, who really started the ball rolling. He was born in 1793 and in a fantastic career went on to ride 16 Classic winners, including the 1,000 Guineas and the Oaks, five times each, the 2,000 Guineas four times and the St Leger twice.

It's interesting to note that at the end of the 1972 Flat Season John Day's space-age relation had won 17 Classics, including six Epsom Derbys.

One of the biggest gamblers in John Day II's time was Lord George Bentinck. He was prepared to lay out thousands even in those days. He was a great character, the like of which we do not see on the racecourses today.

He put a few horses with John Day II, who took out a licence to train while he was still riding. He opened up a few horse-boxes and started operating from Danebury, near Stockbridge in Hampshire.

It was a happy partnership, Lord George put his money down with fearless abandon and John Day II produced the winners. But like so many friendships in racing it all blew up over a lost gamble.

In 1843 Lord George's colt Gaper was entered for the Derby. His owner backed the horse as though he was the only one in the race. But John Day II wasn't quite so keen on their chances.

He couldn't quite see the colt as a Derby winner and as he exercised and galloped the colt at home he became more and more certain that he was entering a loser. And being keen to make a few pounds when the opportunity presented itself, he started laying the horse to lose a small fortune at the very same time as his lively owner was making hefty wagers with nearly everybody in sight.

Eventually the news got out and Lord George got to hear of his trainer's actions. In an angry rage he insisted that all the horses were taken away from Danebury, including the unfortunate Gaper, who true to John Day II's predictions did run unplaced in the Derby.

John Day II may have come unstuck with Gaper, but he later went on to train Pyrrhus the First and Cossack. It was when he moved to Findon that he really started making a name for himself, mostly while he trained for an astute moneylender called Henry Padwick.

Mention Findon to anyone connected with racing now and they'll tell you about one of modern-day racing's great characters, Captain Ryan Price, the trilby-topped ex-commando who has produced controversy and winners from his Findon yard with the same regularity in recent years.

But in the 19th century it was John Day II who was making the Sussex locals dance for joy. And the big coup came in 1854 with a filly called Virago, who as a two-year-old had looked very moderate when running unplaced in a seller at Shrewsbury the previous year.

Racing experts were rather surprised when John Day II entered Virago for the City and Suburban and the Great Metropolitan and also entered the filly for the 1,000 Guineas.

The two Epsom handicaps, still a major feature of the racing calendar, were both run on the same day. In one of the most remarkable efforts of training known to the Turf, Lester Piggott's forerunner trained the same filly to win both these races within half an hour of each other. And then she went on to win the 1,000 Guineas as well. So Lester Piggott is not the only one in his family who has been capable of the near impossible.

John Day II's son, John Day III, took over at Danebury

17

while William, another son, had started turning out winners from Woodyates in Wiltshire.

When John Day III's daughter, Kate, married top jockey of the day Tom Cannon, Lester's ancestors were getting a rich line of racing talent on the same family tree.

Cannon became one of the greats of racing. In 32 years he rode 1,544 winners, including the 1882 Derby winner Shotover, the 2,000 Guineas four times, the 1,000 Guineas three times, the Oaks four times and the St Leger once. He took over at Danebury as the main jockey from George Fordham, who was another man with a terrifically successful record in the saddle, being champion jockey 14 times.

Cannon was a rival of Fred Archer and they had many superb clashes which led people to believe that there was not much to choose between the two experts. Archer was champion jockey from 1874 to 1886, often topping 200 winners for a season.

His Classic record certainly shows his brilliance must have been something quite out of the ordinary. He won the 2,000 Guineas four times, the 1,000 Guineas twice, Derby five times, Oaks four times and St Leger six times.

When John Day II died in 1882 Tom Cannon moved into the Danebury stables and started training. He, too, was a great success. And besides sending out several big Flat race winners, he also trained the 1888 Grand National winner Playfair.

Mornington, Kempton and Tom were Cannon's sons and he also had a daughter called Margaret, 'Morny' was champion jockey six times and Kempton won the Derby on St Amant in 1904 at 5–1. Tom carried on this seemingly endless line of successful jockeys, but switched to training at Compton in Berkshire.

It was the daughter Margaret who next played the vital role when she married Ernest, the son of a well-known Nantwich farmer in Cheshire, Tom Piggott.

Nantwich is famous for its cheeses and formerly for its brine pits. In the history of racing it will be remembered as

18

the meeting place and union spot of the Cannon family with Lester Piggott's ancestors.

The Piggotts had been a farming family for many years, but they also knew the horse world backwards. They were all keen hunting men and besides riding in amateurs' races, also became respected horse dealers.

A foot and mouth epidemic virtually wrecked Tom Piggott's career and he lost all his livestock. Heartbroken, he had to quit the stables for the cellar ... for he became the landlord of the Crown Hotel in Nantwich.

But his son Ernest was not to have his career taken away from horses and he became one of the leading steeplechase jockeys of his day, both in England and on the Continent. The Piggott raids across the English Channel didn't start with Lester relentlessly chasing after Derby winners in most European countries and with his exploits to lift the valuable French races, including the most glittering Gallic prize of all, the Prix de L'Arc de Triomphe. They were started by Ernest many years before. Ernest Piggott won the Grand National three times, on Jerry M in 1912 at 4–1, and twice on Poethlyn in 1919 (incidentally, the race was run at Gatwick, site of the airport now, and was called the War National Chase) and at Liverpool the following year at 11–4. He was champion jockey three times in England and was reputed to have a fearless style which made him a great rider of a finish, something in the style of the remarkable Irishman Jonjo O'Neill, who, if he scents victory, will drive his horse into the last fence at all possible speed. Courage is his password.

Later Ernest turned to the training world with a small yard at Letcombe Regis and continued the family's success in the City and Suburban when he saddled 1923 winner Dry Toast.

Lester's great-uncle was Charles Piggott. He never rode as a professional but was a fine trainer just after the First World War. His stables were situated just a furlong or two from the top bend at Cheltenham racecourse, the Gloucester headquarters of steeplechasing which contains oceans of wonderful memories for National Hunt racing enthusiasts.

Charlie's biggest success came in 1939 when African Star flew over the last hurdle and up the Cheltenham hill to win the Champion Hurdle at 10–1. In the saddle that day was Keith Piggott, Lester's father. Next year they tried to repeat the performance, but were second to Solford, a much-fancied 5–2 chance ridden by S. Magee.

Charlie achieved some fine victories from his small number of horses and Keith Piggott was often the jockey responsible for hefty gambles giving the bookies a financial trimming. Keith was an outstanding horseman. His small, determined frame made him an ideal pilot of the timber-toppers, and between the wars he chalked up over 500 victories. His biggest moment came at Liverpool in 1927 when he triumphed on Trump Card in the Grand Sefton Chase. That was his finest hour at the hallowed Aintree circuit, which has seen so many hopeful contenders leave the tree-lined paddock there and come to grief out on the course at one of the challenging fences, which were much higher and more difficult to jump in those days. Lester's father was one of the toughest little men ever seen on a racecourse.

Keith Piggott was unlucky that he was about at the same time as Gerry Wilson, the partner of the great steeplechaser Golden Miller who, until the entry of Irish wonder horse Arkle, was rated the best chaser of all time. Given a bit of luck on several occasions Lester's father could have been champion jump jockey. He never won the game's most famous prize, the Grand National, as a jockey, but had a never-to-be-forgotten moment in 1963 when he trained Ayala to win a shock 66–1 victory for Mr Teazy Weazy Raymond, the leading ladies' hairdresser.

Keith's brother Victor was no mug in the saddle, either. He pipped his brother by two in 1925–6 when Ted Leader was the champion. He rode more than 300 winners, but unlike his famous modern-day counterpart, was forced to quit riding because he put on too much weight. Unlike his relations he didn't turn to training, but joined his father-in-law, Sidney Moore, in a bookmaking business.

The final piece was added to the jig-saw when Lester's father married Iris Rickaby, whose great-grandfather Fred had trained Wild Dayrell, an even-money hot-shot, to win the Derby in 1855.

Grandfather Fred won the 1896 Oaks on Canterbury Pilgrim, a mare who became one of the founder members of the Stanley House Stud, controlled by Lord Derby. The leading light of the Stanley House stables in 1971 was the world's record yearling buy, Crowned Prince, who cost 510,000 dollars and was at one time Lester Piggott's biggest Classic hope for 1972.

Iris Piggott's nephew Bill became one of the leading jockeys after the war until he retired in 1968. He never won the Derby, but would count the 1,000 Guineas as his favourite race. He was twice second, on Unknown Quantity in 1949 and two years later on Subtle Difference. But in 1961 he scored a brilliant win on Sweet Solera at 4–1. He also won the 1967 Eclipse on Busted. He was to become an assistant stipendiary steward at the Royal Hong Kong Jockey Club, a position which reflected the immense respect he commanded for the straight qualities he had gained over years on the Turf. Sadly, in 1970, he was forced to give up the post after a terrible car crash which left him with serious head injuries.

So there you have it. Lester Piggott was born into a family bursting at the seams with racing heritage. And in later life, of course, he married Susan Armstrong, the popular daughter of Sam Armstrong, who has trained a host of top-class winners. Susan, like Lester's mother, has won the Newmarket Town Plate, the only Flat race for female jockeys until 1972 when the Rules of racing were changed by the Jockey Club. Susan also became one of the shrewdest buyers ever at a sales ring when she formed her bloodstock agency.

With all this background Lester Piggott *had* to go into racing. It was in his blood, stretching back to the 18th century when John Day operated at Mere. Perhaps with so much talent in the family he was even scheduled to become champion jockey one day. But it was Lester Piggott's own amazing brilliance that was to stamp him out in front of his forefathers, and every other man who has ever ridden a horse. His talent was inborn. His genius was unique.

CHAPTER THREE

The 'sensible little boy' wins at Haydock

'He had to be a jockey and before he was able to run around I can remember him saying, "I'm going to be a jockey, I'm going to be a jockey".' The small man sitting in front of me with a weathered face, jockey's legs and an impish little grin every few moments looked up proudly at the striking colour painting hanging above the dining-room table ... and well he might.

For this was Keith Piggott, the cheerful father of the greatest jockey the world has ever known. And who can blame Piggott, snr, for being proud of his family as he gazes up and sees the picture of his son Lester riding the Irish speedster Nijinsky to his 1970 triumph in the Epsom Derby?

As he showed me more pictures of his son in action a hundred memories flashed back as he mentioned Never Say Die, Crepello, Carrozza, Petite Etoile, Valoris, Sir Paddy, Nijinsky, Sir Ivor ... and so it went on. Almost a run-down of all the post-war greats.

'Yes, Lester is the best-ever jockey – nine rides out of ten,' his father told me with typical honesty. 'But with his background there wasn't much more he could be than a jockey, and a great one at that.'

One picture of the young Lester, almost chubby-faced and looking more like a choirboy than a kid destined to become a name on the tip of every race fan's tongue, made my mind switch to another ex-jockey I had visited a few days earlier. High above the horse-mad town of Lambourn stands a magnificent white-painted house. The tiny man

23

with dark glasses and a walking-stick who opened the door to me just three days before Mill Reef's 1971 Derby was Fred Templeman, then the oldest living Derby winning jockey. His success came way back in 1919 on Grand Parade, a 33–1 outsider. Years may have gone by and Fred had had operations on his eyes, but his mind was then as alert as it ever was.

He was only 4 ft 9 in. when he rode his first winner at Gatwick in 1905. Later he had a good career in the saddle and then turned to training. He regarded a jockey's hands as all important and after shaking hands with him it was clear to see where his strength lay.

Looking out across the hills he told me: 'Of course, in my day Carslake, Brennan, Weston and Childs were my buddies. But I always thought that Danny Maher was the best of us. He was such a brilliant judge of pace.

'Our idol was Steve Donoghue. But he was a fool to himself. He won over a quarter of a million pounds. But when he died he didn't have a shilling. I went and saw him and it was pitiful just before he died.'

Fred pointed in the direction of the town when he spoke sadly of fallen idol Donoghue, but he went on to tell of his experiences as a trainer.

'We used to have a lot of gymkhana and local shows,' he told me. 'Suddenly we all became aware that one kid was always winning. His name was Lester Piggott and he wasn't much more than three. At all these functions he'd win the kids' prize. Later, when he was an apprentice, I put him up. I sensed he would be great. He was a very sensible little boy.'

Lester, named after his mother's brother Fred Lester Rickaby, who was killed during the First World War, can look back on a glorious career which has seen him ride probably most of the finest racehorses Britain has produced since the early 50's. And it's fascinating to think that it all began on a little New Forest pony called Brandy, which Keith Piggott 'picked up for a tenner'. When Piggott, snr. took the pony back to his training stables he thought Brandy would be an ideal first horse for his young son, who had already shown that he was keener on riding horses than playing games with the other children.

'He never liked kids' games,' says Keith. 'All the time he wanted to be alone with horses.'

Keith had a bit of a fright when he tried to test out Brandy at home . . . he was thrown four times before breaking him in. There was a long discussion before young Lester was finally allowed to take his first ride.

But his parents should not have worried. Lester got on the pony and rode around the Berkshire yard with the assurance of a master and looked as though he had been on the horse's back a thousand times before. From that moment on the pair were inseparable. It was around this time that his parents discovered that young Lester was partially deaf. 'We found him sticking a radio right up to his ear, although it was fully turned up,' his father told me. Even at this young age perhaps one of the mysteries that make Piggott such an interesting character was beginning to take shape. Playing with other children was boring for him, perhaps the hearing problem making him feel unsure. From the start he became a 'loner'. But once on Brandy's back he was a different person, able to communicate with the pony through the reins and with his hands and feet. There was no embarrassment for him as he took his first steps in learning to make a horse do exactly what he wanted to.

The £10 paid out by Keith was a great investment. The pony, which had previously been running wild in the New Forest, became Lester's stepping-stone towards some of the finest horseflesh the world has ever known. Brandy and young Lester were soon taking part in the gymkhanas around Lambourn and Wantage, where experienced racing men like Fred Templeman first started to spot skills uncanny for one so young.

In 1942 Keith and the late Freddy Fox, who won the Derby on Cameronian (1931) and Bahram (1935) and broke Gordon Richards' long reign as champion jockey for one year in 1930, organized a horse show in aid of the Red

Cross. Lester was just six years old and took part in a race over a three-furlong course with really sharp bends. The age limit was 12 and the course quite tricky for such young riders.

But Lester won with the ease of an experienced rider. Brandy pulled her way to the front and stayed there. Lester just made for the winning post confidently, occasionally looking over his shoulder to see if the older children were going to make a challenge. How many times has Lester looked back on trailing beaten rivals over the years? I wonder.

I don't suppose there was any betting on the race but I know today that if you have backed one of Lester's mounts there is no better sight than to see the champion jockey giving that quick glance over his shoulder as he speeds towards the line. It's a kind of a signal to his followers that all is well and is usually greeted with a mighty cheer by everybody except the bookies, who have probably again had every reason to curse his existence.

Rip and Diana followed in Brandy's footsteps as the horses used as the training ground for future genius. And all the time he had his father instructing him in what he was doing wrong. If he made a mistake, Keith was not the kind of man to mention it casually over a cup of tea. He would bellow across the yard and young Lester would see the situation quite clearly. As the months went by Lester was being schooled by his father into a kind of freak jockey. Soon he was capable of taking on kids twice his age and outpacing them all in terms of skill, courage and even cheek at all the local horse shows.

Before he was seven years old, Lester was seen perched on the top of a racehorse as his father's string went out for their early morning workout across the Downs. A couple of times he ended up on the turf after the horses had done some sudden trick. Lester may have been a little startled, but these were lessons he always remembered and they were a vital practical experience as he set about accomplishing the only ambition he had in life: to be a jockey, but not just another jockey – the best.

The deafness still presented problems and, no doubt, changed his character. While other children enjoyed each other's company and combined games, Lester was the loner. But he never regarded himself as lonely while he had a pony or racehorse to ride.

He went to a private school near Lambourn when he was 11. It was all very interesting to Lester, but his mind was on other things – the horses he had to leave back home every day. But early each morning he was up at the crack of dawn and riding out with the string on the gallops and doing the work of a normal stable boy, including grooming two horses his father gave him special charge of. Then it was a frantic ride on his bike to school. And a hectic ride back to see if he could get in any more riding at his father's yard before the horses were boxed up for the night. Sunset was Lester's saddest hour of the day, for it meant that his love of riding was closed down for a few hours.

By 1948 Lester had become five stone and was ready to make his début at 12 years old in the sport he was later to rule with a vice-like grip for so many years. It's ironic that Mill Reef, Paul Mellon's extra-special horse, should have gone to Salisbury for his first-ever racecourse appearance . . . Lester Piggott did the same.

On April 7th, 1948, he walked out with the rest of the apprentices for a handicap race. He rode a three-year-old filly called The Chase, who was trained by his father. Unlike Mill Reef 23 years later, Lester did not start off with a win. But he got on well with The Chase and his father had no hesitation in putting him up again at Bath, Kempton and Worcester during the summer months. By August Lester was itching to get back on the course.

His chance came in a seller at Haydock on August 18th. Several top-class Northern jockeys thought they had the race to themselves, including 'Cock o' the North' Bill Nevett, and Joe Sime. But as the big boys were fighting it out, Piggott sprang from nowhere and, using brilliant control, beat his rivals by two lengths. The winner's price was 10–1. The winning jockey was 4 ft 6 in. and weighed in at 5 st 4 lb.

Lester doesn't usually smile his head off, even when he rides a Derby winner. But that day the little lad, showing a remarkable skill for a 12-year-old, did have a big grin on his face.

'It was terrific. I rode the last five furlongs hard and managed to pull ahead,' came the after-race quotes from the jockey, who has since won a record eight Derbys and said about as much.

Keith Piggott, who admits that his own interest in the race was not confined to the prize money, beamed like a contented father. The outcome of the race, or the way his son had handled the winner, were no surprise to him. In a classic understatement he told reporters there that day: 'There is no reason why he should not become a good jockey.' Mrs Piggott told the eager journalists ready to break the news of racing's new wonder boy: 'He is just a very ordinary boy.'

That, too, was an interesting statement. For there was nothing 'ordinary' about Lester. Even at this young age he had kidded the opposition, some of them men with hundreds of winners behind them. All the jockeys who took part in that race on that sunny day at Haydock were never to forget the ease with which the kid bamboozled them.

After the race Lester was soon back in the horse-box and heading back south on the 210-mile trip to Lambourn. It was eight hours before he got home and went straight to bed. Early next day he would have to be up and about in the yard, grooming horses before dashing off to school.

That night racing journalists in Fleet Street had the name 'Piggott' on the brain. It was to be a condition known to the scribes for many a night for many a year.

'Boy of 12 beat the jockeys', claimed one paper. But it was discovered that Lester was not the youngest rider of a winner. His grandfather, Tom Cannon, had won his first race when he was nine. Lester Piggott was three years late compared with Tom Cannon. But one message did ring out loud and clear from Haydock that day ... Piggott had arrived. It needed only one winning ride to prove that the legend started way back by John Day was continuing, and it was in young, but very capable hands.

CHAPTER FOUR

'We Piggotts have always thought a lot about money'

Lester Piggott, hailed at 12 years old as a whizz-kid and a new Gordon Richards, ended the 1948 campaign with just the one win on The Chase at Haydock from his 24 mounts. He had two seconds to his credit as well in his already much talked about début season.

But he had presented problems for everybody around him. His father realized that his son had the ability lesser men dream of. And other trainers were constantly ringing Piggott, snr, to see whether they could obtain the youth's services in the saddle. There's nothing a clever trainer with one eye on the form book and the other on a rich handicap likes better than the prospect of putting up a young claiming apprentice jockey who can, by his allowance, make a monkey of the handicap. Piggott, jnr, was just the fellow the trainers wanted. And Lester, driven on by the thought of that one win at Haydock which sparked a 'I want winners' dynamo inside him, yearned to get back into the winner's enclosure. But there was only one problem – school.

Lester wasn't an up-and-coming apprentice who had left school and was making a name for himself in a racing yard. In 1949 he was still only 13, yet the most sought-after rider of the junior brigade. During his second season he had 120 rides, not the major jump in number one would have expected. He rode six winners, eight seconds and 39 thirds. How he wished, as he had to set off on his bike to the local school, that he could skip a couple of years in his life and carry on with the job he was obviously bred to perform ...

taking on and often beating men three times his own age in the tough, gruelling world of Flat racing.

Eventually something had to be done and arrangements were made with the local teaching authorities that Lester would have private lessons. 'If I had a day off from school to go to the races I would put in the extra time with one of the teachers to compensate for it,' Lester explained. When he reached the official school-leaving age of 14 in November, 1949, he was out of the door and away down the lanes on his bike like a greyhound. No more the boredom of sums and history. Now it was to be horses, horses and horses.

Some of his critics point out that perhaps he did not have the fullest education. Perhaps he didn't need it for the way of life he was to make his life's work. But when it comes to sums I don't think that there can be much doubt that Lester is more than capable of working out any financial poser quicker than most men.

So 1950 was the year when the gateway opened on to his full-time racing career. From 120 rides the previous year, he suddenly switched to 404 rides and 52 winners, which made him champion apprentice.

Racing was to see all his iron determination in the final furlong; his never-ending will to win, and his brushes with officialdom which add to the virtually unsolvable make-up of the master's character. When Piggott rode one of his finest races ever in 1970 to win the Derby on Nijinsky, he came back to the winner's enclosure looking as though he'd just received a tax demand for thousands. There was not a hint of a smile on the face once described as 'a well-kept grave'. Later, when Piggott emerged from the weighing room, the Pressmen of the day gathered round him. Making an effort to be helpful he said a few words, very few. When a brave young scribe asked him why he didn't smile he replied: 'I was thinking of all the times Dad said, "Why didn't you win?" '

In a flash I think we saw the true character of this remarkable man. Every minute of the day, someone, somewhere is probably talking about him. He must have more headlines

31

to himself, more pictures in the Press, and spark more debates than all the world leaders put together. Yet nobody really knows him. He remains a mystery. A man with an almost ghost-like character who is not really understood by even his closest friends and relatives. Yet his reply that boiling afternoon at Epsom makes me think that his father, who doesn't believe in beating about the bush, probably had a far greater effect on Lester than any other of the racing men he was later to come into contact with.

Keith Piggott told me: 'We Piggotts have always thought a lot about money. If we had a good bet, we expected to win. There's no two ways about it. Maybe in the old days I was a bit hard with Lester. I'd certainly tell him if I thought he rode a horse badly.

'In my younger days when I was riding if I had been beaten on a horse my family had backed heavily and they thought it was my fault, they would not talk to me for a fortnight.'

This was the atmosphere Lester was schooled in. He quickly learned that anyone can be second. He was taught that to win was the ultimate goal and anything less was failure. When he grew to manhood he confessed: 'If I fail to win a race I always think I've ridden a bad race.'

He started out as an apprentice with five shillings a week pocket money. He read the glowing words of praise that were being penned about him. But he didn't become a big-head, unlike some prospective champions. Whether it was because of his deafness or his upbringing he remained a shy lad, always happy to keep himself to himself. Things haven't altered today when everybody on the racecourse would love to stop and have a talk with him. Lester will never be the chatting champion.

In those early days he had to work hard, extremely hard. His name was being promoted as some sort of super horse-man. But that didn't mean he had to skip the jobs in the yard, all the simple day-to-day tasks that every kid who dreams of being a champion has to start by doing. Lester spent most of his time with horses but at this stage of his life

32

once admitted: 'All horses are alike to me. They all obey the same orders.' And it became quite clear to people watching him go about his work that no horse was likely to get a special stroke in his father's neat, slate-roofed yard – unless they had just won for him. He had an almost cold, remote attitude to the horses he rode in the early days. And the same kind of unimpressed reaction to the rules laid down by the governing body of the Turf. It was to get him into more than one spot of hot water before very long.

In the big Lincoln Handicap at the start of the season Piggott should have ridden Seconds Out for Jack Solomons, the well-known boxing promoter and later in life bookmaker. But he was k.o.'d before he ever got into the ring. Instead of a ride in the Lincoln he had a ride in an ambulance. He was riding the favourite Pandite in a previous race when the horse stumbled and he was hurled to the ground 50 yards from the post. He cracked his collar-bone, but it was a clear indication of just how determined the 15-year-old was when he announced: 'I'll be riding again at Newbury in a fortnight.'

When he won the Kent Handicap at Folkestone on Blue Sapphire it was the 25th winner of his career, and he progressed from 5 lb apprentice to a 3 lb claimer. Incidentally, when Lester recorded this important victory, a milestone in his career, he beat Gordon Richards into third place.

Already he was the new Gordon Richards, and when he beat the old maestro in a tight finish it just added flame to the fire for Pressmen who were making comparisons between the two ... one who had been champion ten years before the other was born. The other still a kid, but greatly angered when he was described as reading comics.

'I much prefer it when I'm racing,' said Piggott. 'I am not keen on lessons. But you have got to learn, haven't you?'

Everybody connected with racing quickly learned that year that the great asset the new wonder-boy had which made him different from the rest was his own remarkable confidence in himself. But this was to have consequences not entirely pleasant for Piggott.

His first suspension came in the early part of 1950 when he finished third on Sailor's Knot at Hurst Park. The stewards didn't like the way he tried to force his way on to the rails and stood him down for 24 hours.

'Boy jockey suspended for day by stewards', rang out the headline in the *Daily Graphic* in July 1950. It referred to Piggott's second suspension, again for 24 hours. He had to appear before the stewards and give an account of his riding of the filly Trumps Green in the last race, the Moderate Plate, when he finished third. They wanted to know in particular what he did during some scrummaging at the bend into the straight. After hearing his side of the story they expressed their disapproval and suspended him for 24 hours. Keith Piggott greeted the news by describing the act as 'boyish exuberance'.

A month later he fell foul of the authorities at Worcester. Quickly, frighteningly quickly, Piggott was becoming the big talking point in racing. And it wasn't all compliments. Basically, he was trying to go for small gaps in the fields. Sometimes the gaps expanded and he went through safely. At other times he was causing genuine danger to himself and other jockeys.

Soon after he had ridden his 40th winner and lost his apprentice allowance he was in more trouble. Australian Scobie Breasley, who was later to be one of his leading rivals for many years and champion for the first time in 1957, objected to him at Newbury. This time the stewards, never men who like regular appearances of a transgressor, stamped on Piggott firmly. He was banned until the end of the season. They explained that it was for his own good and added that he might not see it that way but he would do later on.

That I very much doubt. Yet, only a few hours after learning that he would be exiled from the racetracks until the end of the season, young Piggott was again back in the headlines. His exit from the racing scene was not going to be a quiet affair. In a tremendous battle with Doug Smith on Kelling and Ken Gethin on Valdesco, Lester, riding Zina, flashed

34

past the winning post at Newmarket at the end of a memorable Cambridgeshire. The 14-year-old kid jockey everybody was talking about had taken on Doug Smith, probably the best rider of all time, over the tricky Newmarket circuit and he had no doubts as to the result as he promptly rode into the space allotted for the winner. But the photograph revealed that Kelling had won by a neck with Zina second. Piggott, who had received special permission from the stewards to ride Zina and two other mounts at the meeting, obviously intended to go out on a big-race winner.

He reflected afterwards: 'I thought I had won. Zina had to race by herself. Had there been something alongside us I think she would have pulled out more. When I was going down the straight I thought that the race was in my pocket.' With that Lester tucked his riding gear under his arm and was driven home to Lambourn. Racing was not to see this truly remarkable teenager again that season. Again his father gives the Piggotts' view of the suspensions. 'Lester was only going for gaps that he was entitled to go for. He wasn't using rough riding tactics. Everybody started to pick on him.'

If these cases did upset the Piggott camp perhaps there was some consolation, for there was far, far worse to come. Yet, despite that ban until the end of the season, Lester Piggott became champion of the apprentices with 52 winners, 45 seconds and 39 thirds. He obviously liked the feeling of champion. It was a feeling he was going to have to cheer him many more times in future life.

In 1951 he was champion apprentice again, this time with 51 winners. He had his first big race win in the Great Metropolitan Handicap at Epsom on Barnacle to re-live the success that his ancestors had enjoyed over a century before on the undulating Downs course. He also moved into the big time at Sandown when he won on Mystery IX in the Eclipse at 100–8. He was becoming more and more the punters' friend, especially the housewives'. The post-war years when cash was scarce were beginning to come to an end. Small punters, looking for a new hero, turned to L. Piggott. And they were all rewarded at Kempton when he roared home on a 220–1 double. Not for the last time the bookmakers had to dig deep in their satchels as Piggott dismounted in the winner's enclosure. Yet oddly Lester looked no more happy than the losing bookies. Even on the third day of that season Piggott had given the bookies good warning of his teenage intentions when he rode a double, and one of the winners was 25–1. Nowadays if Piggott rode a donkey in a big race I don't think the Turf accountants would risk those type of generous odds.

As Gordon Richards, the fabulous jockey who ended his career with 4,870 winners and a well-deserved knighthood, had never ridden a Derby winner, the racing Press were quick to dream up an obvious angle. Would young Piggott win the world's best Flat race before Richards? It was the big talking point among race fans. In fact, Sir Gordon, who was known to everybody as 'Moppy' because of his jet-black hair, pipped Lester by one year when he won the Derby in 1953 on Pinza to crown the end of a glorious career. But Lester didn't have to wait much longer. He was first home on Never Say Die the following year, so it was just as well that Pinza did his stuff. But that's another story.

Lester may have been champion apprentice for the second and final time, but again he was not able to ride until the end of the season. Previously it had been the tough line of the stewards that had made sure that he had to stay at home in Lambourn, most evenings reading about the exploits of Fred Archer and Steve Donoghue. At lovely Lingfield – well, it wasn't quite lovely for Lester – on August 25th a horse ridden by Eph Smith fell in front of Piggott near the winning post. The horses were all travelling at such a speed that a collision could not be avoided. And there was a big pile-up. Unlucky Lester again broke his collar-bone and also had two bones broken in his left leg. It was a long time before he was able to have the heavy iron support removed from his leg.

So that was the end of 1951 for the champion apprentice. Injuries, suspensions and masterful victories from a mere schoolboy . . . it's hardly surprising that Piggott was becoming a household word.

During the winter of 1951–2 there was a change in the boy champ. When he reappeared at the start of the Flat season the following year he had lost his midget appearance. Gone were the days of the 5 st tich. Instead he had shot up in height and his riding weight had increased to 7 st 12 lb. By now not only were trainers very anxious to secure Lester Piggott's services as a jockey, but more than one stable wanted the quiet, well-mannered rider as their own property.

Fred Templeman was one who made a bid to secure the riding rights on Lester. But Lester's father decided against the idea and in February it was announced that he would be first jockey to Mrs James V. Rank, whose horses were trained by Noel Cannon at Druids Lodge. The post became available when Scobie Breasley decided that the British climate didn't suit him and returned to Australia . . . but not for long.

Mr Rank had died in January and there was much speculation that the stable might not continue to operate. News that Lester had been booked as Mrs Rank's rider meant that their plans for the summer months ahead were alive and well.

Piggott, who later became the man nearly every stable wanted to ride for them – sometimes no matter what the price – had signed on the dotted line for the first time. But, yet again, banishment and disgrace hovered menacingly round the corner. In the eyes of the racing overlords, young Piggott had not learned his lesson. In Lester's own eyes he was often being victimized because an older colleague refused to give him ground. It could have been that the more senior jockeys resented the success the youngster was getting.

He had become the best apprentice jockey since Frank Wootton, who was champion jockey four times before he was 18. He rode 201 winners even before he was 19. Even in these early days it was becoming very clear that when, or if, Gordon Richards quit it would be Piggott who would be odds-on favourite to wear the jockeys' crown.

The problem of his injured leg was still with him as he set about his new job with Mrs Rank's horses. After the plaster had eventually come off in November Lester said: 'It was agony. I found it very difficult to make my knee bend again.

'I kept having to grab hold of my ankle and pull the leg up under me to make the knee bend. But after a while it did begin to loosen up – and finally it was as good as ever.'

Aware of the public's interest in him winning the Derby before Richards, Lester must have been pleased with the prospect of riding Gay Time. He was a good colt and had run impressively in the 2,000 Guineas at Newmarket, which is the usual yardstick to judge Classic hopes for Epsom, although the first test is over a mile and the second over the tricky one and a half mile Surrey circuit.

But Lester's dream of winning the Derby at the age of 17 was not to be. The man who was later in life to storm past so many men and wreck their hopes had to taste the agony of being runner-up. Two furlongs from the finish Charlie Smirke, one of the greatest characters the Turf will ever see, dashed into the lead on the Aga Khan's Tulyar. Then Piggott made his move on Gay Time, who was a 25–1 outsider. As he drew level with Tulyar his horse, which had been hanging to the left, hung almost into Tulyar's heels, and Piggott had to pull him up slightly. Naturally, he lost a little ground and was never quite able to make it up. His brave effort was thwarted by three-quarters of a length.

But that was not where the race ended. As Gay Time and Piggott went past the post Lester said: 'The horse fell on his head and I had no chance of staying in the saddle.' Like something out of a comedy film, Gay Time cantered off past the enclosures and eventually headed down the main road into Epsom. He was finally caught and returned to the race-course. One person certainly didn't see the joke – Piggott. He had finished second in a race meaning so much to his family pride and history, yet he could not weigh in, because he could not prove that he had been carrying the correct weight in the saddle. When the horse returned the saddle was still intact and so all was well. But before Gay Time could be officially placed second, Piggott had changed his colours for another race.

There was no disgrace in losing to Tulyar, whom the grand old man of the Turf, the Aga Khan, regarded as the best racehorse he had ever owned. His friends warned him not to overestimate a colt who had only done just what was asked of him. This was the Aga Khan's fifth Derby win and as trainer Marcus Marsh put it: 'The bookmakers were clipped for £40,000.'

If Piggott felt a little sick that he had come so close to winning the great prize he really should not have worried. Two years later the glittering prize all racing people yearn to win, from the freckled-faced kids 'doing' the Classic colts to the trainer, the jockey and the owner, was his. And he didn't have to feel any bitterness towards the Aga Khan. For within a few years he was to be associated with the Aly Khan's cracking filly Petite Etoile, who won the Oaks at Epsom. If Lester had known of the money-spinning triumph and big-race glory that was just around the corner, maybe he wouldn't have been quite so determined in those early, formative years.

But there's no stopping a genius when he gets the bit between his teeth.

CHAPTER FIVE

Glory and Shame on Never Say Die

Through the long winter months Piggott rode in several hurdles events. He showed many of the characteristics of his father when taking part in the National Hunt game, but I think that the thought that was foremost in his mind was that Derby defeat on Gay Time.

During 1952 he won £23,390 for his owners. But it would have been a great deal more if he had managed to pip Charlie Smirke on Tulyar. Even at this young age Piggott cursed himself that he had come so near to winning the race of his dreams. In his book he might as well have finished last as second. He yearned to be the Derby-winning jockey to maintain the legend that had gone before him.

Still, as an apprentice the usual riding fee was £5 5s and £7 7s for a win. He also got the usual 10 per cent of the prize money, so it's fair to say that even in those early days Lester was mounting up a nice little sum which is kept by the trainer as trustee until the rider becomes a full jockey. But Keith Piggott added: 'Presents are not always given and travelling expenses have run into a good four-figure sum in two seasons.'

The youngster's wealth was augmented in 1953 when he rode 41 winners from 441 rides. His deafness was now not quite so acute and he had perfected the art of lip reading. He could talk to an individual with ease, but when in a crowd he often still found the situation confusing.

The hurdle riding sharpened him up for the Flat, although like all National Hunt jockeys he got to know the thump of the turf after a fall or two. One resulted in him breaking his shoulder. Shrewd race men thought it was unwise for the apprentice still to take part in hurdles events. 'Surely there are bigger pickings around the corner and he does not want to damage himself?' they said.

The big pickings were not far away, it was true. Lester had ridden a horse called Never Say Die at Liverpool and was not impressed. Only outstanding horses still stand out in his mind and after the first meeting with Never Say Die he certainly was not gasping to ride the horse ever again. When he rode the horse in the Free Handicap at Newmarket and finished down the field he was even more sure that his high hopes of a Derby winner were not going to be answered by this customer in 1954.

Gordon Richards had finally won the Derby the previous year on Pinza. Now Lester was chasing the same goal . . . but not with much confidence in 1954. He heard that Never Say Die's trainer, Joe Lawson, had been contacting several other more experienced jockeys for the ride and five had actually turned down the chance. Finally Lester received a telegram from Joe Lawson saying: 'You ride Never Say Die. Still feel sore about losing on Gay Time to Smirkie?' It was cleverly worded and Piggott quickly accepted.

Almost immediately Lester heard that Robert Sterling Clark's three-year-old was impressing everybody on the gallops at Newmarket. Perhaps he had, like many colts before and after, suddenly matured into a decent sort with a little summer sun on his back. But Keith Piggott, who drove Lester to Epsom that day-to-remember in the family Alvis, recalls: 'He was very miserable on the way to the Derby. When I asked him why he was so glum he just said, "I've got no chance. He isn't good enough." '

The general public must have had the same idea, for when Piggott went down to the start on Never Say Die the odds were 33–1. As far as form was concerned, and even his rider's opinion, he was a no-hoper.

The first Classic chapter of the Lester legend was written when Piggott forced Never Say Die home ahead of Arabian Night (Tommy Gosling) and Darius (Manny Mercer). The kid's big ambition had been fulfilled. But if you had seen the expression on his face as he was led back to the cheering masses in the special winner's enclosure at Epsom you would have thought that he had just been out for a pre-race spin. Ice-cool throughout the race, he was just as unflappable afterwards.

He told reporters: 'Unlike Gay Time, Never Say Die had the speed to stay up with the leaders. Once we straightened up at Tattenham Corner I just went for my life and was finally surprised how easily we overhauled Manny Mercer on Darius and Doug Smith on Rowston Manor.'

When a questioner in the House of Commons that day asked the whereabouts of the Prime Minister he was told: 'Sir Winston Churchill is at the other meeting.' Those who later saw the pictures in the newspapers knew that the 'other meeting' referred to Epsom, where Piggott had picked up £1,600 for 2 minutes 35 seconds' work.

The Prime Minister, like thousands of others, had seen a rare sight . . . a shy, unsmiling lad of 18 winning the Derby. He was so young, in fact, that his father told me: 'We were asked to go to a special banquet in London afterwards. The owner was celebrating, but it really wasn't the kind of party suitable for a youngster, so we declined the offer.'

In fact, Lester was driven straight home and was in bed well before ten o'clock. He had won the world's greatest race, but to him it was just another landmark in his determined bid to join his forefathers as a great name of the Turf. As his parents drove him home they realized that they had reached Reading and he still had not said a word. His mother turned to him and said:

'That must be a wonderful horse.'

'Yes,' came the cold reply, 'but he's not a patch on Zucchero.' Lester was talking about a horse he knew few other men could handle.

Never Say Die, American-bred and sired by the famous Nasrullah, was now a leading candidate for several top-line races. And the biggest disaster of this Derby pilot's career was just around the corner. Trainer Joe Lawson picked out

42

the King Edward VII Stakes at Royal Ascot as the next engagement. It was to be a fated choice for Lester Piggott. His father Keith still recalls the race with much bitterness.

'It wasn't Lester's fault. The television film proves that,' he says, at the same time scotching one of the biggest rumours in racing by telling me: 'I have spoken to Gordon many times about the incident and it's just not true that Lester said to him, "Move over, Grandad, I'm coming through."'

'I think that now Gordon realizes that Lester was not to blame for the incident that day.'

But even now, over 20 years later, Lester is still widely associated with the 'Move over, Grandad' line.

Flashpoint came as Never Say Die hung a little to his left as he went for a gap. At the same time, Rashleigh moved up on the outside with Gordon Richards aboard. Garter was in the centre of the field and was completely sandwiched and had to be sensationally pulled up. Many shocked racegoers thought that Gordon had slightly bored Garter the moment that Never Say Die hung to the left. Rashleigh went on to win, but immediately there was a stewards' inquiry. Never Say Die, the Derby victor and a hero a few weeks previously, had finally finished fourth after one of the most controversial finishes in racing history. Everybody had a different opinion of the event, which is still true to a certain extent today.

But if there was confusion in the racegoers' minds, the stewards were quick to act and once again Lester Piggott was the man singled out as the culprit. After hearing the jockeys' evidence they 'placed the blame firmly on Lester Piggott and allowed Rashleigh to keep the race'.

Piggott was suspended for the rest of the money-spinning Royal Ascot meeting and was also referred to the stewards of the Jockey Club. The second event had a more sinister air about it. It's history now that the Jockey Club banned Piggott for the rest of the season, denying him a victory on Never Say Die in the St Leger. But it will probably never be fully appreciated the bitterness it created in Piggott's mind.

Having seen the films and spoken to other jockeys I can only say that the ban was too harsh. Lester's record was not good – he had been in several similar instances – but on this occasion he may well have been so harshly punished because of his record rather than the events which turned the racing world upside down in the final two furlongs in the Ascot straight that day.

Years later, when Lester was asked about the incident, he said openly: 'When we got near home I thought sure we would win. I could see my cousin Bill Rickaby on Garter and could see he was beaten.

'I made for a move outwards and at the same time Gordon made his effort on Rashleigh. I am sure that Gordon's horse bumped Garter on to me. The bump put us out of the race. If there had been a camera patrol in operation in those days it must have been that the stewards must have put down Gordon as well.'

The day after the incident racing was still buzzing with talk of the Never Say Die performance. Would the stewards really stamp down heavily on Piggott or would they listen to his side of the story? As I have said, the stewards acted fast and harshly. They put him out of the game for the rest of the season and also suggested that he moved to another stable not controlled by his father. Keith Piggott felt terrible about this aspect and told me years later: 'I remember Eph Smith coming in one day and saying, "Keith, your lad is going to end up seriously hurting somebody." But I knew that he was going for gaps that were his right. The trouble was that there were too many old jockeys about who should have packed up years before.'

To this day Piggott still feels that he was terribly wronged by the stewards, who, it seems, were trying to be over-severe as a warning to Lester for the future. At Epsom, Lester was on top of the world, although he never showed it. After hearing the stewards' verdict he was very downhearted, but being poker-faced can have its advantages. He was able to hide his torment, although anybody with a scrap of intelligence must have known the agonies he was going through. He was especially upset as he was on the verge of his 300th winner and thought that there was no better place than Royal Ascot to reach this total. He had several fancied rides, including Bitter Sweet and March Past. Keith Piggott told Pressmen at the time: 'Lester is heartbroken. His whole life is racing. But I keep telling him that six months will seem nothing when compared with his tremendous future in the game.'

Lester went to work for Jack Jarvis at Newmarket as a stable lad. It was a spell of his life he tried to forget, but I imagine that he can never forget the months of non-racing. Perhaps he needed a lesson to reduce his excessive will-to-win, but the ban caused nothing but resentment because of the incident it stemmed from. 'Six months' bloody hard labour and less than a fiver a week for serving it,' was how Lester summed up his sadness. And perhaps it was the financial aspect that angered him as much as the loss of big-race glories. By now he was earning a huge sum for an 18-year-old and the thought of the flow of cash being cut off made the whole incident doubly painful.

But perhaps the bitterest pill he had to suffer was listening to Charlie Smirke glide Never Say Die home by an oh-so-easy two lengths in the St Leger at Doncaster. He had spoken to Charlie Smirke on the telephone and offered advice on how Never Say Die would be best ridden. Smirke took the lead two furlongs from home and opened up such a clear advantage he was nearly able to canter home.

In September, 1954, owner Clark announced that Never Say Die would be retired to stud immediately and that he would stay in England for the next four years. Lester can look back at the horse in two ways. It gave him that never-to-be-forgotten moment of glory over the Epsom winning line with all the high-class rivals behind him . . . and also let him know what it's like to be in the racing wilderness and back as a humble stable lad. But it was typical of Lester's tough-as-teak determination that he got down to his new job well. There was to be no bad behaviour and he impressed Jack Jarvis with his work in the yard.

Racing is a funny game sometimes. The future can often look so rosy, and yet end up as black as thunder. Likewise, sometimes the very worst seems to be on the cards but suddenly everything changes and your greatest hopes are fulfilled. So it was to be for Piggott. On September 23rd the Jockey Club lifted their ban on him, cutting short the suspension by three months. It must have been part of the punishment that they did not restore his licence until after the St Leger.

When Lester came back he had a problem which he was to come face to face with even more in later life . . . weight. His inactivity on the racecourse had resulted in his weight going up quite appreciably. He was only given a few days' notice of the ban being lifted.

But he returned with a lesson learned. He said at the time: 'I'm coming back a little more wary. Any more trouble might see me suspended for life.'

Like all good stories the Never Say Die suspension had a happy ending. On his first day back Piggott rode Cardington King to victory in the Isleham Stakes at his now local Newmarket track. Racegoers at the headquarters of the Turf need a human interest angle or the appearance of a truly magnificent horse before they go into raptures. But that day, as Lester stormed clear coming out of the Dip and went on to win by half a length, they did let their hair down. And as Lester returned to the winner's enclosure there was a small hint of a smile on his lips. Back among the rivalry and competition he loved. Back among the only life he knew. And back in the place he yearned to be every half an hour throughout the summer afternoons – the winner's enclosure. He loved it.

And that wasn't the only good change of fortune for Lester. He ended that season with 42 winners from only 262 rides. His win per cent was up almost double on the previous year, and he was tenth in the jockeys' list despite his suspension. He was really being noticed by the men who mattered, including the Newmarket trainer who was later to combine with Piggott as one of the greatest racing double acts of all time, Noel Murless.

Murless, the Newmarket overlord and the trainer who made perfection his password, was suddenly faced with the prospect of finding a stable jockey. Gordon Richards – by then knighted – had received a bad injury when the Queen's filly Abergeldie fell on him and dislocated his pelvis. He was in hospital for several weeks after this accident which happened at Sandown in July, and finally decided to call it a day. So Murless was on the lookout for someone to replace Richards, who rode 4,870 winners in a brilliant career which saw him champion jockey 26 times. People in racing spoke openly that one day Lester Piggott would succeed Richards and Murless must have also highly rated his talents because he offered him the job as top jockey at the fabulous Warren Place Stables, where the material was all gilt-edged. After his retirement in 1976, Noel was subsequently knighted and handed over Warren Place to his son-in-law Henry Cecil with a reputation for straightness seldom rivalled in racing.

Among the impressive list of Murless's owners was, of course, the Queen. To be offered this type of post by Murless obviously meant that the leading men in racing thought that Piggott's restless days were over and he could now set out on a new, more controlled part of his career. They were dead right. There were to be the occasional skirmishes with the stewards. Many, many times he was to dismount from a horse and be beckoned into the stewards' room. But for a magic spell Murless and Piggott were to break all records in British racing. Murless took a slight gamble when he offered the job of replacing Sir Gordon Richards to a youngster who had just come back from a hefty ban. But Piggott didn't let him down.

CHAPTER SIX

Crepello wins in Classic style

Joining Noel Murless's all-conquering Newmarket yard was another vital move in Lester Piggott's clear-cut path towards greatness. From 1955 until 1966 the Murless-Piggott duo was the most feared partnership on the Turf. They were an ideal couple. When Murless had moved down from the North he was hailed as the one man in racing likely to become a champion trainer. By the middle fifties Piggott had emerged as everybody's idea of the next champion jockey.

But in 1955 Doug Smith took the title for the second successive year. Lester's rides went up to 530 and he eventually finished up with 103 winners – topping the elusive ton for the first time. He was fifth in the jockeys' table and among his many successes was a fine victory on Darius in the Eclipse Stakes at Sandown at 11–10. He was also second in the St Leger on Nucleus behind the Boyd-Rochfort-trained Meld, who completed the 1,000 Guineas, Oaks and St Leger treble.

Doug Smith had a great year with 155 winners. The youngest son of a Shottesbrook (Berkshire) farmer he, like Piggott, had a deep racing heritage in his blood. His middle brother Eph was a top jockey and won the Derby on Blue Peter at 7–2 in 1939.

In fact, as Eph recounted to me: 'I told friends of mine the year before that only one thing would prevent me winning the Triple Crown on Blue Peter . . . Adolf Hitler. And I was dead right.

'Blue Peter won the 2,000 Guineas and Derby, but war

broke out just before the St Leger was due to be run and so I missed the chance. He was a certainty.'

Doug Smith, who once had a losing run of 111 consecutive defeats, joked: 'Steve Donoghue once did worse – he had a losing run of 112.' He was especially masterful at Newmarket and the 1955 season was well remembered for the terrific duels between the experienced Smith and the still young Lester.

'A nice chap – but pretty tight with his money', was how one writer referred to Smith at the time he was champion. But it was a reputation for being keen on money that was to become Lester Piggott's trademark. Father Keith Piggott told me with a cheeky grin: 'We Piggotts have always thought a lot about money. Perhaps I'm the easy-going one. When we had a bet we expected to win and we have always regarded money as a very valuable object.

'I remember in my younger days riding a horse in the North. My uncle, the trainer of the horse, and myself kept things pretty well to ourselves and we agreed that on this particular day this was going to be the big occasion.

'As I went out to the paddock to ride the horse I saw my father and told him that I thought it was a good thing. He duly dashed off to back it and the horse later obliged. My father came into the weighing-room and told me that he had won £80 for £2. He was highly delighted and told me that he'd give my uncle and myself a taxi ride back to the station to save us getting the tram. It was a special treat.

'When we got outside to the taxi rank my father was trying to make one of the drivers take us to the station for five bob, although the fare was 7s 6d. He went all along the line asking them, but none of the drivers was prepared to do business.

'So in the end my father refused to pay the full fare and we had to go on the tram. It was full of racegoers and some of them were pretty rough characters. My father was so worried about the type of people on the tram and the £80 in his wallet that he went the entire journey with his arms closely folded and hugging to his coat, afraid that somebody should pinch the money.

'Maybe Lester's inherited this love for money.'

When he first went to Newmarket to do his stable job with Jack Jarvis, and later when riding for Noel Murless, he had digs with his two 'aunts' – 'Squiff' Rickaby, who was the father of jockey Bill Rickaby, and 'Boie' Lane, who was the wife of well-known jockey Fred Lane, who won the Derby on April the Fifth way back in 1932. It was while he was here that Lester's great love of money became very evident. In a wonderful chapter entitled 'My Cousin Lester' in his book *First to Finish*, Bill Rickaby gives an insight into the ways of Lester. Says Bill frankly: 'Lester relishes every crisp fiver like some rare jewel, for money is his staff of life and he ekes it out as sparingly as a man faced with fifty years of unpensionable retirement.

'Modesty always was the major part of his make-up. Petulant and precocious at first, perhaps, he would never shoot his mouth off in a boastful way.

'A more maddening weapon which he wielded unmercifully as an apprentice – and I think unwittingly – was complete disdain for those who tried to help him in the vital, formative years.

'After he had gone for a gap that was not there, I would tell him, "Lester, that was very dangerous." He would look into my thundery face and without so much as an apology would carry on changing his silks for the next race. Lester only took advice from his father.'

Bill Rickaby also recounts stories which show how much young Lester was counting pennies even in those days. Once Bill's mother told him: 'Do you know, Bill, I think Lester is mending his ways. He bought me a lovely bunch of flowers today.' But later Mrs Rickaby rang Bill to tell him that Lester had taken the cost of the flowers out of his rent. He also thought that if he only spent a couple of hours in his bed instead of a full night's sleep he should not pay the full rate.

Other jockeys tell stories of how even in those days he would always seem pretty careful with his money. It was usually agreed that when jockeys took it in turns to drive to meetings together the man doing the driving would pay for the petrol. But Lester would ask: 'Can somebody lend me two quid for the petrol?'

Another Rickaby story concerns an incident at London Airport after he and several other jockeys had just returned from a riding trip. 'We were a long way from the airport park,' says Rickaby, 'and I was just about to get aboard a bus when Lester pulled me back and said, "I'll get a taxi."

'We climbed in with two others and asked to be dropped off at the car park, leaving Lester to carry on to the main building alone.

'As we got out Lester said, "Let's have five bob each for the fare." We coughed up and as the taxi drove off, I noticed there was only 2s 6d showing on the meter. I noticed, too, that Lester was laughing like a drain in the back of the cab.'

There's no doubt that some of these incidents could not happen to any other jockey. They would get tremendous stick from their colleagues and have to pay up sooner or later. But not Lester. From a very early age he had this way about money. Like the previous Piggotts he knows that he wants success on the racetracks to bring him in more loot . . . and he means to keep hold of it whenever possible.

Life at Warren Place meant plenty of winners and plenty of cash for Piggott. By 1956 he had lifted his winners to 129 from 642 rides. But he still had to be content with third place in the jockeys' championship with Doug Smith again champion with 155 wins.

In 1957 the position changed, and it was Scobie Breasley, the wily Australian who had returned to England, who topped the list with a magnificent 173 wins. In third place? Yes, it was Lester again, this time with 122.

But this was to be the year of Crepello and another Classic triumph for Piggott.

By the early spring of 1957 Newmarket's busy horse-mad gossips were whispering only one name . . . Crepello. The previous year had seen patient Murless give the colt an easy

51

time. It was not until the day of the 2,000 Guineas at Newmarket that Sir Victor Sassoon's Crepello was ever asked to pull out all the stops. But already Crepello was firmly established locally as the Classic horse of the year for the Murless-Piggott duo. Backed down to 7–2 Crepello was highly impressive as he beat Quorum (Russell) and Pipe of Peace (Breasley). And racing discovered that if Doug Smith was the master of Newmarket, Piggott had become a very good second best over the course.

The Rowley Mile looks the easiest course in the business. It's as wide as a football pitch and as straight as a Roman road. But it contains many little tricks and setbacks. The day Crepello won demonstrated that Piggott had learned all there was to know about it. And he had to hang about for an agonizing five minutes as the start was delayed. Just as the flag went up at the top of the rise to show that the horses were under orders, Irish-trained Chevastrid showed what he thought of the whole venture and threw Jimmy Eddery, father of Pat Eddery. The jockey of Dovasbere was also thrown, so there was quite a delay. Chevastrid bolted off across the heath and as handlers tried in vain to recapture him Piggott remained cool on the much-fancied Crepello.

Eventually the race got under way and Crepello, who had the worst of the draw, being placed on the outside, was turned into the stand rail by Piggott, who wisely showed that he did not intend to make a run on his own in the centre. From the stands it looked as though Piggott had given up valuable lengths and it was a long time before the Sassoon colours could be seen at the rear of the field. At the Bushes it was clear that Piggott's plan was working perfectly as he made his way through an already tiring field. As he met the slight rise in the ground three furlongs out he must have realized that Scobie Breasley and Pipe of Peace were going well. When they dashed down into the Dip they were joined by Tyrone, who was ridden by Frenchman Poincelet. Tyrone started to go to the right just as Piggott prepared his final burst on Crepello. Poincelet's whip was flashing dangerously close to Crepello, but eventually as the pace quickened Piggott eased Crepello and in the end, as he stormed away to win by half a length, it was Free Handicap winner Quorum who had made the greatest challenge, with Pipe of Peace third a head away.

Sir Victor Sassoon was not at Newmarket that day. He was in Nassau. He missed a really mature display from Piggott, who later said: 'Crepello was a great horse. He won the Guineas copybook and did what I wanted. I didn't have to ask for anything.'

After the Guineas triumph Crepello's next target was, of course, the Derby. And as Lester was driven to the undulating Surrey circuit on June 5th he was a lot more confident than the youngster who had been driven from his Lambourn home three years earlier to ride outsider Never Say Die. Now Crepello was all the rage. The nation had taken Piggott and Crepello to their hearts and the fact that he was 6–4 favourite showed that many of them planned to take the bookmakers to the cleaners, which is always a very unlikely state of affairs.

In 1953 Sir Victor Sassoon had the great joy of seeing Sir Gordon Richards win on Pinza after 28 attempts to break his Derby duck. It seems unbelievable that a top-class champion like Richards should have to wait so long. Yet he said frankly: 'I often made the wrong choice and had to sit back and watch horses I had won on, winning the Derby.'

Piggott never had these worries. Second while still in his teens, a winner at 18, now he was going to make it a double at 21. And he did it in the fastest time since Mahmoud in 1936.

Again Piggott had a bad draw, but rode a perfect race. Murless had done his share of the work by sending the colt to post looking every inch the best three-year-old of the day in Europe. Both Murless and Piggott believed that only ill-luck could wreck their dreams. A cold wind whistled around Epsom that day and the crowd jostled to find a warm corner. A far, far cry from the sweltering days later in Piggott's Derby career when you could have fried an egg on top of the stands as the brilliant sunshine shone down on Sir

53

Ivor and Nijinsky. Again Crepello had to wait at the start as it took three attempts to get the horses under way. Drawn No. 2, Piggott needed all his mastery of the Epsom track to make up for a bad start. If he had been caught napping he could have been cut off from the front runners and would have had to surrender valuable ground. But right from the start it was possible to see him sending Crepello to the near front of the field. At the two-furlong stage he was fourth and bang on the rails – the very position he wanted. Masterful! As the field swung round Tattenham Corner Crepello was tucked in just behind the leaders. Ballymoss, Laor, Chevastrid and Eudaemon were the leading runners at this stage.

The electric atmosphere must be at its peak as the field speeds down the hill and round Tattenham Corner. As Crepello was such a hot favourite and the bookies were laying 10–1 bar, everybody's glasses were fixed on the figure of Crepello and Piggott. Once in the straight, unruffled Piggott allowed his colt to join the leaders. A mighty cheer went up as Crepello went clear, for the crowd realized that he was still on the bit.

The chestnut with a white blaze on his face had done it, although Vincent O'Brien-trained Ballymoss (T. Burns) and Pipe of Peace (Breasley) were not outclassed. It would indeed have been a terrific achievement if Vincent O'Brien had trained the winner of the Derby so soon after switching from being the wizard trainer of the jumps, winning the Grand National for three successive years.

But for O'Brien the disappointment was brief. His turn was to come. And the unsmiling man on the back of Crepello as he was led in to tremendous applause was to play the vital role in the not-too-distant future.

But on this day it was Noel Murless who celebrated his first Derby victory. He had trained the winner of the St Leger and 1,000 Guineas and twice lost the 2,000 Guineas by a head. Now it was his turn to enjoy the excitement of being a Derby trainer, although anybody who knew his perfect horsemanship was aware that it could only be a matter of years before it happened. For over a year he had regarded

Crepello as a likely Derby winner. Sir Victor Sassoon's colt was described by Murless as 'one of the kindest horses I have ever trained'.

Sir Victor often had to watch races from a wheelchair. But on this occasion, with mighty cheers ringing in his ears, he walked from the members' enclosure with the aid of a stick down to the course and led Crepello into the winner's enclosure. He stood smiling by the side of his horse, which he had bred himself, and joked with reporters: 'This has taken more out of me than it has the horse.'

For Piggott it was a moment of great happiness. It was to be only the start of a Classic onslaught by himself and Murless. The wonder boy who had been treated in the recent past like a truculent child had shown that at the age of 21 he had obtained horse skills and jockeymanship far in excess of his tender age. Reporters of the day likened him once more to Richards and Donoghue. On this Derby performance it was hard to argue against him being put on such a high pedestal.

Later that year, at Royal Ascot, his genius came shining through like a bright light. Riding 6–1 chance Zarathustra, he displayed a powerful finish which captured the Gold Cup. These were happy times at Ascot for Lester, who had known the most wretched days of his highly publicized career at the Royal bonanza.

Crepello was aimed for the St Leger to attempt to become the first British horse to win the Triple Crown since Bahram in 1935. But he was also entered for the richest race on the English calendar at that time, the £30,000 King George VI and Queen Elizabeth Stakes at Ascot on July 20th.

On the very day of the race, Sir Victor Sassoon came away from a three-cornered talk with Noel Murless and Lester Piggott. 'Not going,' was his shock announcement. Odds-on Crepello was withdrawn because of the heavy going. All had looked well and it seemed as though it would be a good day and the going suitable for Crepello. But there was a torrential outburst and a miniature river ran down the covered way from the course to the station. Sir Victor was pressed for an announcement, but waited until Piggott had ridden Aorangi in the first race. The clouds had lifted when the big discussion took place. But Piggott was obviously worried about Crepello's likely performance in the heavy going and recommended that the horse be withdrawn.

CHAPTER SEVEN

'Confidence in his own genius'

'I have seen him ride hundreds of winners, but without doubt the greatest single race I ever saw him win was on Carrozza in the Oaks in 1957 – he was brilliant. No other man who has ever put his leg over a horse's back could have won on her that day.'

This is Keith Piggott, Lester's father, talking about the way Lester won the fillies' Classic at 100–8 for trainer Noel Murless. It was a super show as he pipped Silken Gilder and Rose Royale II. Ironically, it was not until 1970, when Piggott had a chance ride on the Peter Walwyn-trained Humble Duty, that he won the 1,000 Guineas at Newmarket over the Rowley Mile at the first spring meeting at headquarters. But long before that, in countless races, Piggott had shown that he had a special gift with the ladies! Whether they were temperamental fillies or lazy ladies, they were handled with superb jockeymanship by Piggott.

I asked another top stylist Jimmy Lindley which of all Piggott's displays impressed him most. He thought for a while and then answered in his usual intelligent fashion: 'I think of all the rides I have seen Lester have, the way he used to ride Petite Etoile was the most impressive. She was not a true stayer, but Lester seemed to be able to perform magic with her.'

In 1958, although he had 83 winners, Lester was not able to capture the Classic glory he had come to know at such a young age. He had just as many rides as in previous years, over 500, but for only the second time in a sensational spell from 1955 to 1971, he was not able to top the 'ton'. He slipped to fifth in the jockeys' championship.

But 1959 saw his wonderful display in the Oaks on Petite Etoile. The filly had won the 1,000 Guineas at 8–1. Incidentally, the jockey of the third filly in this race was Australian George Moore, who rode Paraguana. He was a rider who was to become far more accustomed to Newmarket before long, and Lester Piggott was indirectly to be the reason. As Lindley so rightly says, Petite Etoile was probably not an ideal Oaks horse, but Piggott rode a perfectly timed race to get her home in front of Cantelo (Eddie Hide) and Rose of Medina (Ephie Smith) at 11–2.

The year 1960 will go down in Turf history as the beginning of Lester Piggott's vice-like grip on the championship. From 640 starts he rode 170 winners and was champion for the first time, clearly following in the footsteps of the great riders in his family who had walked before him. History was repeating itself.

The highlight came at Epsom on Derby Day when he gave Sir Victor Sassoon his fourth Derby in eight seasons, his previous heroes being Pinza, Crepello and Hard Ridden. For Piggott it was a hat-trick of Derby victories, and he said afterwards 'This was by far the easiest of my three triumphs' as he described his win on St Paddy.

The St Paddy Derby will go down in racing history as the hoodoo Derby. When St Paddy beat Irish colts Alcaeus and Kythnos the race was over, but the peculiar incidents before and during the race were a talking point in racing circles for weeks to come. While exercising on the Epsom Downs to get fully tuned up for the world's top Classic and to get accustomed to the oddities of the Epsom track, Irish horse Exchange Student dramatically broke a leg the day before the race and had to be destroyed. Then during the race, the red-hot favourite, Angers, the French champion, smashed a leg and had to be put down. French jockey Gerard Thiboeuf told the Stewards afterwards that no one was to blame for the sensational tragedy that left thousands of punters with useless betting slips in their pockets. Angers was racing by himself when the colt's fetlock snapped about five furlongs from home. It is highly unlikely that Lester Piggott gained his third Derby win because of this injury. St Paddy was always going well and Piggott's statement that it was his easiest Derby victory was certainly justified. Quickly on to the scene to see Angers was the course veterinary surgeon, Mr J. Garrett, who had the unfortunate task of destroying the favourite. Later he said: 'I was following the runners in a car and came upon Angers, who had been pulled up and whose jockey had dismounted. Angers had sustained multiple fractures to the near foreleg including the cannonbone, fetlock and pastern. There was no hope of saving him quickly.

'It was amazing that a horse should sustain such injuries when galloping. It can be done when the horse is off balance.'

The small race field of 17 runners was the lowest since Pearl Diver and G. Bridgland at 40–1 defeated 14 opponents in 1947.

I love the story of the young unmarried Lester pressing the head porter of the Rutland Arms, Newmarket for the use of a bedroom for a short time in the early spring of that year. 'That will be a fiver,' said the porter when a smiling Lester emerged. 'I'll do better than that,' said our hero. 'Back St Paddy for the Derby – he'll win.' The porter forgot the fiver and had £10 on St Paddy. The price at the time, before the season had even started, was 66–1.

When racegoers assembled for the St Leger at Doncaster later that year the events of the Derby may well have been in their minds. St Paddy, the Derby victor, appeared on the book to be a certainty for the last Classic of the year. But whether the non-challenge of the favourite at Epsom affected the odds or not the starting price of St Paddy at 6–4 on was rather generous. With his form behind him and Piggott in the saddle it seemed more likely that 9–4 on would have been a more realistic offer. St Paddy was the Classic winner nobody seemed to want to back. Perhaps the fact that Piggott had never won the St Leger after several healthy attempts was one of the facts that affected the price.

But St Paddy won the Leger with almost cheeky ease from Ireland's Die Hard (8–1) and Vienna (20–1). The French-trained Anaram II started at 9–2 second favourite, but was an utter flop. It was a slow-run race, but Piggott coasted home by three lengths.

With this display St Paddy silenced his critics, who had been very reluctant to acknowledge his Derby triumph as a great success. Besides being Piggott's first success in the St Leger it was also the first time that wealthy owner Sir Victor Sassoon had won the one-mile, six-furlong contest. For trainer Noel Murless it meant that for the third time in four years he had won more than £100,000 for his fortunate patrons. The St Leger first prize in those days was £30,378.

After St Paddy's win, Sir Victor Sassoon stated that his horse would be kept in training as a four-year-old and would have the Coronation Cup, the King George VI and Queen Elizabeth Stakes and the Arc de Triomphe in Paris as his long-term objectives.

Off Key, St Paddy's stable companion, started off in quick style in an attempt to make it a fast-run race with a good gallop. But the pace was never really very fast and the time was, in fact, 12 seconds outside the Doncaster record.

Eph Smith on Off Key was closely followed by Spartan Green and Sir Winston Churchill's Vienna. Just over two furlongs from home Piggott and St Paddy cantered into the lead and from that point the race was all over. Vienna, a very popular runner in Sir Winston's pink colours with chocolate sleeves and cap, ran on courageously for his third place.

Piggott summed up the race: 'I could hardly help going to the front halfway up the straight. I had time to look over my shoulder three times and the only horse who ever threatened to make anything of a race of it was Die Hard.'

It was not to be the last time Piggott turned the St Leger into a one-horse affair by a long way.

In July, Piggott had been involved in one of racing's biggest upsets for years. Racegoers and punters stood in near disbelief at Ascot after the £25,000 King George VI and Queen Elizabeth Stakes when Petite Etoile, the flying four-year-old filly, had gone under to Aggressor by a length. By this time racing on television was becoming one of the regular enjoyments for sportsmen. A huge crowd had gathered at Ascot and there were millions of viewers eagerly watching to see the previous year's Guineas and Oaks heroine in action. Bookmakers, a rare breed who sometimes don't appreciate the sense of occasion, were not in a generous mood to celebrate the appearance of the top-class filly. They yelled, 'I'll take 5 to 2', and got plenty of customers who defied the never-back-odds-on rule to try and cash in on this super performer.

For 10 furlongs of the 12-furlong race Petite Etoile was last of the eight runners. But the punters were not too worried. Anybody who had been at Newmarket or Epsom the previous year must have thought that it was only a patient Piggott sitting at the back waiting to let the filly click into top gear. When Piggott switched Petite Etoile from the rails to the outside the Ascot air was ready for a mighty yell as connoisseurs and gamblers heralded a great horse winning a big race. And as Piggott passed the French and Irish entries it looked as though the odds would be easily landed. But that famous flourish which had destroyed previous rivals with such ease was not to be found. Aggressor stayed on grimly and despite Piggott's all-action finish it was Jimmy Lindley who proved the master of the day.

The wonder filly was retired to stud. She won over £60,000 in her ten wins in 13 races. Her other defeat as a four-year-old came when she was beaten in the Aly Khan Memorial. The going was too heavy and Piggott was never able to produce the usual blinding run.

'Petite Etoile did not really stay,' Piggott reflected afterwards. 'But she had an incredible burst of speed. This ability to paralyse anything in a burst of 100 yards can make both a horse and jockey look the best in the world.

'But I should have won that race at Ascot. I took what I thought was the best way home but I left a little bit too much to do. We were dead when we got near the post and did not have enough to catch Aggressor.'

Lester has often commented that: 'Every time I'm beaten it is a bad race in my book.' Perhaps when he looks back on that Ascot race he still curses a little. To have been beaten by such a short distance is annoying enough. But to lose a race and know in yourself that you really could, or should, have won it is doubly frustrating. At least Piggott is bold enough to admit that he should have won and does not try to hide the true facts beneath the camouflage of excuses used by so many racing people.

Besides being champion for the first time in 1960, Lester had another reason to celebrate. One of the many Newmarket trainers who had been keen to use young Lester's talents when he moved there permanently to join Noel Murless was Sam Armstrong the highly successful trainer from St Gatien, Newmarket. Armstrong, like Piggott, was a name full of racing history. Sam had taken out a trainer's licence in 1923 after being a pupil with H. L. Cottrill at Lambourn. He served with his father, Bob Armstrong, and had ridden 50 winners during a career under National Hunt rules from 1921 to 1924.

When Lester Piggott married it was odds on that it would be to a young lady with a racing background. Susan, Sam Armstrong's only daughter, was the ideal match, and they were married at St Mark's, North Audley Street, in London. Yet again Piggott racing legend was following in the steps of his predecessors and marrying into another family closely connected with the Turf.

But anyone imagining that the Lester Piggott wedding was a big function with hundreds of racing celebrities attending could not be more wrong. In fact only 38 guests attended, and Sam Armstrong explained at the time to the society columns, 'They wanted it quiet. If we had organized it differently we would have had to invite everybody.' Twenty-five-year-old Lester wore a blue striped suit to the wedding and 20-year-old Susan cut the three-tiered cake, decorated with horseshoes and horses. It was a typical wedding between two racing families. John Sutcliffe, later to make a very positive mark in the game as a trainer at Epsom, was Lester's best man, and he proposed the toast to Mr and Mrs Piggott at Brown's Hotel. One thing about the occasion is certain – Lester picked a winner. Susan not only became the mother of his two daughters, but racing manager-secretary for the superstar. She has booked his rides and has been an essential partner in Lester's amazing success.

When Lester set up home in his house (called Florizel) just off Newmarket's busy High Street, Susan became a vital person in his world as a top-flight jockey. Numerous 'phone calls had to be answered. Then, like now, it was often the attractive Susan who helped him with his riding plans. She came from the ideal background and there is no doubt that she has played one of the biggest parts in his march to great-ness. Besides which she has also shown that Lester isn't the only one in the Piggott household who can be a success in the saddle. Susan has won the Newmarket Town Plate and people are quick to remember that Lester's mother, the former Iris Rickaby, had also won the race in impressive style.

Champion at the age of 25 with three Derby victories behind him … that was Piggott in 1960. I think that his forefathers would have been proud to have seen the way the new member of their great set was going about his business. Halfway through the season Sir Gordon Richards, now set up as a trainer, had commented: 'If Lester were only seven pounds lighter he would win the title. Now I doubt whether he will do it.' But Sir Gordon was proved wrong. Lester had only started his almost unbelievable battle against the scales – but he had won. And it was Sir Gordon's jockey, Aussie Scobie Breasley, who was pipped into second place.

Eleven years later – and ten championships later – Sir Gordon told me: 'By resisting the temptation to eat and by depriving himself of all other good things in life Lester showed the most amazing strength of character. The secret of Lester in those early days was his confidence. Confidence in his own genius. For he is a genius just as Steve Donoghue was before. From the very beginning of his career he seemed to know exactly what to do, and when to do it.

'When he had that fine win on Carrozza in the Oaks he stole the race – the other jockeys didn't know what was happening. He just waited for precisely the right moment and then went.

'There's just no doubt about it. From the moment he came into racing it was very clear that he'd got that certain something the others hadn't got.'

Yes, by the tender age of 25 Lester Piggott had joined the exclusive club of outstanding jockeys. He had a long way to go to beat the Classic record of Buckle with 27 wins. The achievements of Archer, Donoghue, Richards and the other supremos still looked like an unclimbable mountain in front of him. But he had made a fabulous start. Retained by the man he called 'the greatest trainer of them all', Noel Murless, and happily married, Piggott set out to develop from wonder boy into wonder champion. Only the fact that his tall frame meant that he had to waste heavily to get down to 8 st 6 lb, and that often his daring riding tactics left other jockeys staggered and stewards furious, stood between him and the title of the 'greatest jockey of all time'.

But this was to be yet another battle in which Lester Piggott was to prove the master by a distance.

CHAPTER EIGHT

'Forceful but never cruel'

Loved by punters, from the housewives with their sixpence each-way bets to the real professionals living in the heaven of tax-free winnings, and wanted by almost every trainer in the land. That was the new champion, Lester Piggott. But there was a brigade in racing who did not look so kindly on his actions. To many people who saw him go for small gaps, urging horses over the line with one dynamic burst and powerful use of the whip, Piggott was a far cry from the genius true racing people believed him to be. He was, in many people's opinion, a cold, whip-happy jockey prepared to go to any extremes to be the first past the winning post.

By now the Press world was keen to gather round Lester. He was the champion and big news. As many people in racing had before, the Press found that the response was non-existent. He clearly didn't want to communicate with reporters and often wasn't prepared to waste more than two sharp words to express his feelings. And when he caused the wrath of officialdom he often showed the same air of disdain. Success and passing years had done nothing to make Piggott more approachable. Shoulder-shrugging and tight lips were his password. Some people put his reluctance to communicate down to his deafness. Others were less charitable.

If Piggott was not keen to communicate off the course he was certainly not failing to get his message over once the gate had gone up for races. His cousin Bill Rickaby observed at the very time when Lester was accused of over-whipping horses and plain cruelty on the racetracks: 'His father Keith taught him to be a man when he was still a boy. Some of the tricks he pulled off on the course would have been better kept until he had mastered the basic rules of jockeymanship.'

In 1961 Piggott rode 164 winners but was not champion again. His biggest success came in the St Leger when he repeated his previous year's success on St Paddy by winning the Doncaster race on Aurelius. For the next two years he escaped the Classic roundabout and had 96 and 175 winners, but still the championship went elsewhere.

Lester always claims that he would have had another Derby triumph in 1961 but this time the most repellent aspect of racing, the cancer of the sport – dope – beat him. 'Pinturiscchio had run fourth in the 2,000 Guineas,' said Lester, 'but he was a long way short of his best that day. Everything he did at home suggested that he would win at Epsom. But I went to his box to do work and found him helpless. The Derby favourite was out and he never raced again. People who dope horses should be shot.'

In 1963 the public's view that Piggott was using the whip too often gathered momentum. The climax came when Casabianca won at Newbury. In stepped a new body to voice their protest at the way Piggott was winning races – the R.S.P.C.A. No other jockey in the history of racing had ever caused such a general outcry as this. The Society alleged that Piggott had 'soundly thrashed' the winner.

Noel Murless, Piggott's trainer at the magnificent Warren Place yard at Newmarket, has rarely taken sides in any controversial issue since he reached the top of his profession. But he did come quickly to Piggott's defence. He said at the height of the rumpus: 'Lester Piggott is not a cruel rider, and he never has been. I hate cruelty. I would never tolerate it with one of my horses. He certainly isn't the ruthless rider he has been accused of being.

'There were criticisms after Casabianca's victory, but he was a very lazy horse. When he gets to the front of the field he thinks that the race is over and won and there is nothing left to do.

'Piggott gave him a smart slap on the hind quarters where it doesn't hurt, and the horse surged forward, more in surprise than anything else. That was all.'

I remember seeing Piggott at his powerful best at Brighton. He did use the whip regularly during the final two furlongs on a two-year-old ... and he won the race by a neck. It is true that the horse looked apprehensive about life afterwards. 'He'll never win again,' a loudly dressed holiday-maker opined in my ear. 'Look, he's flogged the bloody animal to breaking point.' For the record I should add that this horse went on to win several races.

It would also be foolish to imagine that every time Piggott brings the whip down by the horse's quarters he is, in fact, giving his partner a reminder. This is not so. Jockeys have a rhythm as they ride a finish and it helps to let the horse know that he may get a backhander if he slows down. Many times I have seen horses appear to have been clouted by Piggott come back without a mark on them.

But was he really cruel in those early days? Lester said at the time of the fuss: 'Old ladies tell me that I'm cruel to horses because I hit them too hard. Because I flourish the whip a lot and look to be going to use it people get the wrong impression.

'I'm sure Scobie Breasley hits them as hard as I do at times. But he does it in a quiet fashion. No one who loves horses as much as I do would deliberately hurt them. It's just that some are lazy and won't do their best without a crack or two.

'Horses go well for me and I haven't known any go sour on me. We have a different style to the Australians, but that doesn't mean there is anything wrong with it. We are better horsemen than the Americans.

'I know I've had a lot of suspensions, but I've been unlucky. Every time newspaper fellows are short of news I seem to do something wrong. There are times that I am scared to cross the road in case I get knocked down and make the front page.'

Forceful but not cruel ... that was Piggott's defence to the charges laid at him for excessive use of the whip. And it's hard to see a man like Noel Murless, who represents the very best in British racing, siding with Piggott if the accusers were correct in their opinions.

During these years the Piggott magic flowed happily, apart from the odd brush with the stewards. Perhaps we should have remembered those words from his early days which the young Lester ventured soon after his first win at Haydock: 'Horses go soft if you make pets of them.'

Gordon Richards found Piggott a fair opponent. He said: 'None of the rough riding was deliberate. It's all part and parcel of his genius. He just knew that he had to be in a certain place at a certain moment in order to win.'

If Piggott was finding the stewards difficult men to get on with because of his high-speed skills on the racecourse, he was having the same trouble with the police about his speedy driving on the roads. In the space of ten years he committed ten motoring offences. On one occasion he was stopped as he went down the wrong way in a one-way system. When asked for his name he replied: 'John Brown – you've heard of me.' But he gave his correct address in Newmarket. Twice he was fined £50 for speeding and eventually he suffered a six-month ban. During this time he engaged a chauffeur and rarely drove to meetings. 'I've given up fast cars,' he said with a grin. But it was not to be the end of Lester the highway speedster.

Jockeys, of course, can't bet in Great Britain. But I can reveal one bet that Lester had – and, strangely for a man who usually knows all the form, this was a loser. While staying in Chester for the big meeting he bet a fellow jockey £5 that his first child, due at that time in May, 1961, would be a boy. But for once Piggott made a mistake and his wife Susan gave birth to a girl, who was later christened Maureen. The day of the birth Piggott was involved in the kind of rumpus which seemed to plague his life at the top. At Chester that very same afternoon he had ridden odds-on favourite, Pre-emptive in the Grosvenor Stakes. He was involved in a mêlée of horses with Doug Smith, Harry Carr and Scobie

Breasley near the finish. All the jockeys were shown a film of the incident, but it was Lester who was called before the stewards and cautioned.

Had Lester been allowed to bet I'm sure he would have lost another bet that year. He was riding St Paddy, his Derby and St Leger victor, in the King George VI and Queen Elizabeth Stakes at Ascot in July. Now a four-year-old, St Paddy was the acknowledged champion of his age in England. Like Petite Etoile in the same race, nobody could really see St Paddy being beaten, and the money poured on the Noel Murless-trained favourite. But in the paddock those of us who watched St Paddy got a bit of a shock. He swished his tail angrily and Piggott needed all his superb handling to steady his Classic winner. It was the French 2,000 Guineas and Derby winner, Right Royal V, who stole the show before the race. And he went on to do it after the race had started.

As the field swung into the straight at Ascot, the grave-yard for so many big hopes and dreams, Roger Poincelet was sitting quite motionless on the French champion. But so, too, was Lester Piggott who obviously thought that he had plenty of power in the machine room. A furlong from home Piggott drew his whip and tried to lose Right Royal V, but to no avail. The French colt sailed past him and went on to win by three lengths. It was an outstanding training success for French wizard Etienne Pollet and one which they still recall with justifiable pride across the Channel when they remember the outstanding French riders who have scored at Ascot and Epsom. 'Great St Paddy meets his master,' screamed one headline I saw that day. But it could have been that the weight assessment of 9 st 7 lb for St Paddy was just a little too much. Lester, obviously, was aware of this big burden, because when the field went down to the start I noticed that, as there were quite a few minutes before the start of the race, he dismounted so that his mount did not have the task of carrying the weight longer than necessary.

But, generally, these were happy times for Piggott and

Murless – the ideal combination of a superb trainer and world-beating jockey. In racing it's hard to imagine a more suitable double act. Little wonder that so many runners in those money-spinning years started at such short prices.

By now Piggott had become the most talked about jockey in the world. Racing experts openly compared him with the big names and many thought that he was a better jockey than Sir Gordon Richards.

Keith Piggott put an interesting theory to me just after the 1971 Derby when he said: 'I have always maintained that Lester was a better jockey at the age of 18 and for a few years afterwards than he is today. I think all the suspensions haunt him. He knows that if he does anything wrong the racing world is ready to get after him. It's a fear he lives with all the time.'

Perhaps it is true to say that Richards emerged as a supremo during a period in racing history when there were several top-class jockeys about. Fred Templeman told me: 'In my day we had a dozen men who could be picked out as outstanding. Today we only have one – Piggott.'

Richards had to beat the massive talents of Donoghue, Elliott, Carslake, Bullock, Weston, Wragg, Fox, Childs, Perryman and Beary. To take on these kind of rivals and emerge as the best of them showed the ability of the man.

In Piggott's times we have not really seen such outstanding horsemen. Doug Smith was a genuine champion, of course – and it's unlikely that we'll ever see a better jockey round the Newmarket circuit. It was a sad day for racing when Smith decided to quit and we lost the sight of his skill.

In recent years Willie Carson and Pat Eddery have been champions. But they would be the very first to admit that they can't equal Piggott.

Scobie Breasley was always a true rival for Piggott. His strong point was his ability to produce a storming finish that was almost designed to result in a photo-finish. It is possible that he has been in more racing photographs than anybody – and I'll bet was out in front more times than not.

In recent years new jockeys have emerged to rival Piggott.

But he certainly has not had the challenges that Richards was forced to contend with. Richards' strong point was that he rarely lost a race that he should have won. He was consistent, and if the horse was the best in the race he won on it. I like to think that Piggott, while occasionally riding an ill-judged race, will win on horses that no other jockey in the history of the Turf would have won on. And it does seem that if Piggott rides a bad race it sticks out clearly for us all to see.

Richards and Piggott had styles of their own. Many people thought that Geoff Lewis was getting more and more like Richards, but nobody will ever copy Piggott successfully. Young Lewes trainer Mick Masson, the son of the late Tom Masson – one of racing's outstanding characters – has very clear-cut views on would-be Piggotts.

He told me: 'Youngsters try to copy Piggott nowadays, but they are ruddy crazy. He rides so short, but he gets away with it. He balances himself to perfection. But others who try to ride like him have no control of the horse whatsoever. If the horse takes a strong tug at the reins they've had it.'

In the Piggott-Murless heyday it was obvious that Lester had one advantage over Richards – a temperament which doesn't seem to alter at any time. It could be a 'seller' at the old 'Ally Pally' track or the Arc de Triomphe – it's all the same to Lester. Only once or twice in over 20 years of competitive race riding with just about every jockey in the country yearning to show him a trick or two and wanting to finish in front of him have we seen any displays of temper. His is the ideal temperament for a man at the top of the tree, and the big-race atmosphere is something that brings out the very best in him. Crowds and noise worry some horses and men. To Lester, as he is led out of the paddock and on to the course, the thousand eyes on him are all part of the occasion. But they have little to do with his first priority of winning the race.

Sir Gordon Richards, who once told me 'I was born 20 years too soon' as we discussed the big-money rewards jockeys can obtain nowadays, was not quite the same kind of man. Of course, he didn't sweat and panic at the thought of riding in the Derby. But, perhaps, he thought about it more and that may have unbalanced his genius. In contrast, Piggott is at his best in the big races, ice cool at all times.

It's not a coincidence that Richards won one Derby and 13 other Classics. Piggott's record is superior, and on Sundays he often wins foreign races as easily as most people carve the weekend joint.

Perhaps it is true to say that Richards will always be regarded with greater affection than Piggott by the public. Richards was closer to the hearts of racegoers. Piggott remains many punters' idol, but the relationship is based on the cash rewards his success can bring. If Piggott had a genial personality he would nearly be able to walk on water in most people's eyes. But then he wouldn't be the Piggott we know, and the mystique of his character and the unknown depth of the man would no longer hold us like a spellbound audience.

I think that history will show that Piggott would have beaten Richards in a photo-finish for the rider's crown. His record shows that he has few equals. His determination to deny himself the fruits of life which he could well afford shows his strength. Those years working so closely with Murless, a man who can be placed as highly as Piggott in his own field, meant that a little more racing heritage and brilliance was rubbing off on Piggott.

And the fact that it made him restless for even more success did not come as such a shock for those who know Piggott's will-to-win.

CHAPTER NINE

Murless and Piggott agree to differ

Seven Classic winners, four jockeys' titles for Lester Piggott, and for Noel Murless as leading trainer a still unbeaten record of stake money won, the £145,727 in 1959. These were the fabulous facts behind the Murless-Piggott partnership. It seemed the most outstanding partnership between master trainer and super jockey in the history of the Turf.

But as Piggott's success story went from one big win to another he was, in reality, changing the whole face of the game. In days gone by jockeys were little men with little standing in the game. They were simply needed to get on the back of the horse and were very much the servant of the trainer who, in the past, had often been a son of great nobility.

Piggott smashed a class barrier. He became bigger than the game itself. Mightier than the leading trainers, not at all outclassed by the wealthiest of owners. Perhaps one of his greatest achievements was that nobody in racing referred to him as 'Piggott'. He was 'Lester' to everybody and there wasn't an owner in the land who did not love to see him walking into the paddock wearing his colours. Piggott had brought a whole new dimension to the sport. He held the racing world in his hand and cashed in accordingly.

And as the years went by with Noel Murless he realized that there were even more glory and cash rewards to be obtained – if he could go on a semi-retainer. He wanted to ride the cream of the Warren Place yard, the Murless super stars, and all the other top-class rides that he had only to pick up the 'phone to obtain. Piggott was in a powerful position and he knew it.

Eventually the storm clouds between Murless and Piggott gathered. His cousin Bill Rickaby always knew that one day it would happen. He says: 'Lester's break with Noel Murless was, I suppose, inevitable. Lester wanted to have his cake and eat it. He wanted to ride for the country's top stable without a contract, leaving him free to choose rides as he pleased and, therefore, getting the choice of the horses from Ireland, France and England. Lester always wanted to be independent for he was a law unto himself.'

The initial breaking point came when Vincent O'Brien, the wizard trainer from Tipperary in Ireland, contacted Lester by 'phone one day and down a crackly line asked the champion if he would ride his Valoris in the Oaks. Piggott asked Murless to be released from riding the Newmarket-trained filly Varima. Murless, naturally, pointed out that as Piggott was his stable jockey with a retainer, he must stick to his stable mount. Piggott virtually killed the 11-year-old bonanza they had enjoyed by insisting that he rode Valoris in the Oaks, which he did. The result was an extremely easy Oaks win for Piggott in 1966. This gave him a healthy taste of things to come. And when he also partnered Vincent O'Brien's black Pieces of Eight to victory in the Eclipse and Champion Stakes his mind was made up. Pieces of Eight's double was worth £54,298 alone, and the quick cash brain of Lester soon realized that even without his substantial retainer from Noel Murless he could still make very large sums out of the racing game.

He longed for the day when he could study the form book, pick out the horses with the best form, and then contact the trainers and offer his services. There were very few men in racing brave enough to turn down his request. For probably the first time in the long history of the Turf a jockey was dictating to the rest of the profession.

By July the rift between Murless and Piggott was alleged to be over. In fact, I think that Noel Murless would have

74

been prepared to forget everything. He said: 'The differences between Lester Piggott and myself are over and he will resume riding for the stable soon.' During the break Piggott kept his lead at the top of the jockeys' chart. After 140 winners in 1964 and 160 in 1965 he was determined to retain the title and still increase his total of winners. While he had not been riding for Murless it was Australian Scobie Breasley who had taken his place. Who knows that perhaps while Murless had Breasley riding for him he liked his style of Aussie riding? Perhaps it was something Murless kept in his mind for future reference.

Towards the end of the 1966 season Piggott really turned on the style and eventually ended with his best ever 191 winners from 682 rides. But one ride he had at Ascot had more importance than, perhaps, any other race in the year – and, for once, Piggott made a totally wrong judgement on a horse. He rode a two-year-old for Noel Murless at Ascot called Royal Palace. When the race started it was obvious Royal Palace had been left several lengths behind. I can remember looking towards the back of the field and seeing Piggott some six lengths adrift of the others. When they swung into the Ascot straight it was still clear that the champion had a great deal to do. But, then, with one electrifying burst, he went round the outside of the field and then shot to the front. He then went on to win with great ease. It amazed me how he had been able to find the speed to go past all the other two-year-olds while taking the furthest way home from the start of the straight. It must have startled the stewards as well, for they announced an inquiry. They finally confirmed that there would be no change in the result. They had obviously had to examine the possibility that Piggott and Royal Palace had cut back across the rest of the field too quickly.

For my money, slightly enhanced by this odds-on speculation, this was a terrific show. But years later I learned that Piggott himself was not quite so happy about it as one might have imagined. Keith Piggott told me: 'When Lester came back on Royal Palace that day I said to him, "You'll win the Derby on that horse next year." But Lester replied: "No, I won't. He hasn't got enough guts." '

It was a rare boob. And it's certain that if he had dreamt that Mr Jim Joel's Royal Palace was to produce the three-year-old form he did Lester would never have finally ended his contract with Noel Murless. Piggott, possibly the finest judge of horseflesh the world has known, did make this error and it cost him the one gem in life he yearns for more than anything else, a winning ride in an Epsom Derby.

Lester made a second attempt to come to terms with Murless. But the trainer was not prepared to let Lester ride for him without a contract. I think, too, that Mr Jim Joel probably refused to engage Lester without a contract. It's easy to understand both points of view. As I have said, Piggott had reached the position where he had chances to ride top horses outside the Murless yard. He cursed the fact that he had to ride the lesser Murless horses in races which he knew he would have won for other trainers. 'Lester didn't mind the best horses, but he obviously hated the chances of turning down winning rides in the very same race,' his father told me.

Murless was in a difficult position. Technically he had a contract with Piggott and could possibly have been more forceful about the situation. But that is not the man's style. He accepted gracefully and had one ace up his sleeve that Piggott could hardly have foreseen.

It was at the very end of the season that Piggott and Murless finally parted. By this time most jockeys had been retained for the next season by their respective trainers. There were no top-class jockeys available to fill the No. 1 job in English racing. But Murless knew that Australian George Moore might be a possible replacement. He contacted the Piggott of Down Under and discovered that he might be interested. Moore immediately contacted Piggott and asked him what the situation was. All this time Piggott could hardly have believed that Moore would actually give up his life in Australia to come to England. I think that

Piggott hoped that the situation he had longed for was about to happen. He would be able to ride the Murless cream and still be able to pick up the rides he fancied elsewhere. He didn't think that Royal Palace would win the Derby, but he knew the Warren Place yard would be bursting at the seams with talent if previous years were anything to go by.

Of Murless, Piggott openly admitted: 'He's the best trainer I've seen. The way he trained Crepello was a wonder. He won the Guineas and the Derby when he was only just sound.' There's no doubt that Piggott did not want to leave Murless. There was a little goldmine right on his Newmarket doorstep.

It must have been a big shock to Lester when Murless announced that George Moore would be coming over to England in 1967 to ride as his top jockey. If Piggott was being slightly greedy he learned very early on in his free-lance life that Murless, despite all the glory they had shared in the past together, was one man who was certainly not prepared to play ball with him. If Piggott had hoped by his actions to keep the Murless top rides and still be a freelance he had failed badly. It made his start as a freelance all the more difficult. In fact, wherever he turned for advice he was told not to go freelance. It was virtually unheard of at the time. Keith Piggott told me: 'When Lester asked me what I thought I told him not to leave Mr Murless. But Lester was determined and I knew that he would sort the problem out.'

Piggott was now to set out on a new career in racing – one which would pave the way for a complete change-about in the system of jockeys. He was to be retained to ride certain horses of special calibre. His burning ambition and restless energy meant that he was to set out on a new path. He was, of course, the only man who had the determination and confidence in himself to even think of it. He had walked out of the best job and was just relying on his own genius to get a living. Just how popular was Piggott? He was very soon to find out.

Being jockey with a stable like Murless and being a brand-new freelance were two entirely different walks of the game. If Piggott had a bad run in the old days he could fall back on the big stable which was bound to strike form sooner or later. There was always the steady flow of untried talent just waiting to be seen on the racetracks. But Piggott now walked alone. His own exceptional ability was now going to be needed more than ever. Critics of the game mostly thought that Lester had made a big mistake. They just could not see that Piggott would make a successful freelance. Perhaps they all forgot the man's amazing strength of character and his love for racing. Ever since he stepped down from The Chase at Haydock way back in 1948 Piggott had been forced to overcome one crisis or another. He had made a bold break with tradition, but the thought of 10 per cent of prize money and the chance of international rides were his spur. It seemed likely that his total number of winners might go down. Scobie Breasley, riding as well as ever, was everybody's idea for the championship in 1967. Others just hoped that Lester knew what he was doing. It was reported that George Moore picked up £25,000 in bonuses alone in Australia. Obviously, Noel Murless had been forced to offer Moore a massive retainer to lure him to England. Bookmakers immediately offered Piggott at 3–1 against for the championship the following year. But just as Piggot had been wrong about Royal Palace, so, too, the bookmakers had underestimated the magic of Piggott.

A year later he was champion, a freelance champion with 117 winners from 557 rides. Yet again, Lester had proved everybody wrong. And Royal Palace had done the same to Piggott.

CHAPTER TEN

Missing out on Royal Palace

When Lester Piggott turned freelance in 1967 all his closest friends, the very few men he was prepared to turn to for advice, warned him that to break with Noel Murless was, perhaps, a hasty move. But Piggott bravely stuck to his guns and that spark of genius inside him was, yet again, to carry him to new heights of greatness. The previous year he had ridden 191 winners from 682 rides. In his first year as a freelance his win total was reduced to 117 winners from 557 rides. But he was still the champion.

At one stage of the season, when Australian Ron Hutchinson set a blazing pace in the jockeys' championship, bookmakers hastily offered good odds against Lester making it four championships in a row. They should have known better.

Piggott proved in 1967 that he was a genius, able to sling aside the massive support of Noel Murless's stable and still ride more winners than any other jockey. Now his super riding meant everything. He was reliant on other trainers realizing his ability and wanting him to ride for them. The telephone never stopped ringing. And when Lester had a quiet moment he would consult the form book, spot a horse with a likely chance and then contact the trainer. There was never any question of Lester staying at home waiting for people to contact him – he chased rides and his knowledge of the form book was almost unbelievable.

The Duke of Norfolk's trainer, John Dunlop, who topped the list of winners trained in 1970 after a neck-and-neck battle with Doug Smith which ended with him winning by one winner on the last day of the season, always has a kind word or two to spare about Lester. On a visit to his lovely yard in the grounds of Arundel Castle one day I started to discuss jockeys with John. 'Hutchinson is ideal for me and I am very glad that I have got him. He comes down at the start of the season and stays here while he rides the two-year-olds. I don't think there's a better horseman about,' he told me frankly.

'What about Lester?' I asked. John then went on to tell me stories of how the 'phone had rung late at night and it was Lester asking him whether he was going to run a certain horse at a certain meeting in ten days' time. 'Piggott had looked through the entries and seen that I had runners at two meetings. He worked out that Ron would probably be riding at one meeting and was keen to get the chance to ride the other one. Actually Lester is very good. Several times he has gone out of his way to contact me to get a ride and they have always gone close or won. I don't think anybody knows the Racing Calendar better than the Duchess of Norfolk. But this man Piggott certainly does not miss much.'

Dunlop also related to me the occasion when Piggott was riding for him in France one Sunday. The Norfolk party, Dunlop and Piggott all gathered at Gatwick Airport ready for the trip across to France. Says Dunlop: 'I can remember Piggott arriving and saying, "Wall Street is down." It was virtually all he said the complete day. But I think stories about his meanness are perhaps built up. I think that he's rather like American comedian Jack Benny. He knows he has a reputation for being a little mean and so he plays up to it.'

From John Dunlop down in his stately surroundings in Arundel to trainers in the North of England the Piggott pattern was the same. If they had a likely winner in a yard he wanted to be on it. The fearless freelance was in business and he wanted everybody in racing to know about it.

Bill Rickaby, one of the men who warned Lester of the dangers of going it alone, says: 'Going freelance was a very brave move and there were times during the first season that Lester had second thoughts about whether he had done the right thing.'

Father Keith Piggott told me: 'I advised Lester against going freelance, but I should have known that he would make a go of it.'

Actually, Lester's gamble of going solo did not start on the racetracks of Britain. He went 'down under' to come up smiling. He rode two of the three big races in Australia before the British season got under way. Having scored in Australia's international events Lester acquired a taste for his new job. Not even when Piggott had a losing run of 31 rides near the start of his freelance career did he worry. He had ridden four winners in the first few days of the English Flat Season. Everything looked rosy. Then came this bad run and there wasn't a critic, bookmaker or fellow jockey not guilty of wondering whether Lester had made a full-sized boob. But says Lester: 'Other people were more aware of my failures than I was.'

By the end of May, 'Hutchie', as he had come to be popularly known in Britain, had gone clear at the top of the jockeys' chart with 26 winners. But the new freelance was by no means out of it and had scored 20 successes.

Perhaps the most unhappy moment for Piggott, a man who never shows his emotions at any time, came in the first big meeting at Newmarket. It's certain that Piggott must have cursed himself when he saw his Warren Place replacement, George Moore, score a brilliant double in the 1,000 and 2,000 Guineas on Fleet (11–2) and Royal Palace 100–30). These must have been moments when even the calm of Piggott's mind must have taken a hammering.

It's easy to say that Lester must have dashed the quick trip back to his Newmarket home and added up the cash rewards that he had missed by leaving the Murless stable. Perhaps Lester did make a mental note of what money he had already lost by making his decision. But I think that what probably annoyed him more was just the sheer joy he had lost through missing out on the big races. He says: 'Of course it was galling. I had ridden both these horses as two-year-olds. I knew how good they were.'

Royal Palace, the horse Lester had scored on as a two-year-old, was now the likely favourite for the Derby. Mr Joel's horse had won the Guineas in fine style and George Moore started out on a memorable year. He just couldn't do anything wrong. His winning rate was about 33 per cent which is way above the normal average. He was, of course, helped by the fact that the very year after Lester had parted company with Murless, the Newmarket trainer had one of the best years a trainer has ever enjoyed.

While Murless and Moore scooped the big prizes, however, Piggott was still in the limelight. When, let's face it, since he started way back in 1948, has he ever been out of the glare of publicity and controversy?

In May, an attractive three-year-old, Ribocco, had run a poor Derby trial at Lingfield. I remember remarking to a friend at the time that this horse would stand no chance in the Derby against Mr Joel's Royal Palace, but that he might produce his best displays towards the latter part of the season. For once I was bang on the ball. Royal Palace duly continued the Murless-Moore bonanza and won the Derby at 7–4. But it was Ribocco who came second and looked on Derby Day as if he had plenty of room for improvement. And this was where a new trainer on the scene, Fulke Johnson Houghton, emerged as a man with obvious capabilities and a man who was to be closely connected with Lester, the freelance.

Johnson Houghton had served with Major John Goldsmith – a man who had landed a considerable gamble after Piggott had dieted on an orange a day in his younger days to make the weight for a bookie-bashing pounce – and John Cunningham in France for short periods. Now, with Ribocco, he was on the verge of giving Lester the chance of getting back into the big-race glory he was so experienced at capturing.

Pony-sized Ribocco left his Blewbury stables in Berkshire in July to attempt to improve on his Derby second. As

Piggott had been well beaten on Pink Gem in the Oaks by Pia (100-7), he was extremely keen to steal a big-race prize.

The Irish Sweeps Derby at the Curragh was to be his first big success as a freelance. And what made it especially pleasant was the fact that he beat George Moore on the Noel Murless-trained Sucaryl into second place. And the two Australians, Scobie Breasley and Ron Hutchinson, who were making life for Lester tough at the top, were beaten into third and fourth places on Dart Board and Gay Garland.

I was at the Curragh and will never forget the finish to the race. As Piggott stormed to a length victory I'll bet that only a few of the crowd in front of the V.I.P.s' enclosure were watching Lester's triumph. They had turned their heads and had been watching the antics of one of the racegoers who was jumping up and down with excitement as her fancy, Ribocco, turned up trumps. The attractive lady who nearly stole the show was Jackie Kennedy, later Jackie Onassis. Also there that memorable day were Bing Crosby and stunning actress Jane Russell.

But my memory is of Lester urging Ribocco to the line ahead of Lady Sassoon's Sucaryl, who had given George Moore one of his many successes when winning the News of the World Handicap at Goodwood over one mile and two furlongs. Starting at 5–6 the combination won just like an odds-on favourite should.

But over at the Curragh, Piggott had stormed back into the limelight, and I noticed for the first time a certain owner whose name was to become such a leading part in racing and also in the life of Lester, American mining millionaire Charles Engelhard. He owned Ribocco and it was not for the last time by a long way that we were to see Lester coming into the winner's enclosure wearing the green colours with the yellow sleeves and scarlet sash.

Royal Palace did not go for the St Leger, but Ribocco and Lester did. It would have been really interesting to see how the form turned out if these two horses had taken each other on at Doncaster in September. When Ribocco had finished fifth in the Lingfield Derby Trial few people imagined that he had such a glittering career just in front of him – second in the Epsom Derby, winner of the Irish Sweeps Derby, and now on the verge of the St Leger. His performances were a fine tribute to young Fulke Johnson Houghton ... and, of course, to Lester, who rode possibly one of the top ten races of his life to get Ribocco home in the St Leger.

It was a dull day at Doncaster, but the display of Piggott was enough to brighten any heart, and not just the local Yorkshire crowd who backed Ribocco down to 7–2 and gave Piggott a real hero's welcome when he returned the victor. Curiously, Ribocco was repeating the performance of the previous year's winner, Sodium, ridden by Frankie Durr. Sodium had failed to win the Epsom Derby, but had gone on to win the Irish Sweeps Derby and then, finally, the St Leger.

Connections of Royal Palace must have been disappointed that the three-year-old did not go for the St Leger as the Derby form worked out well. But one of the first people to congratulate Charles Engelhard after the race was Jim Joel, who told him: 'I'm so glad you've won, because it's wonderful to see the Derby form work out so well.'

In the race the early pace was set by Great Host's pacemaker, Haarwood II. Ribocco was at the rear of the field until the runners turned into the straight. It was a stroke of typical Piggott genius, waiting patiently until ready to pounce with a storming run that left half the field confused and the whole field beaten. It was the Italian runner, Ruysdael, ridden by Ferrari, who looked to have the race at his mercy. Then George Moore (you couldn't keep him out of anything in 1967) moved smoothly with an uninterrupted run on Hopeful Venture. But from virtually nowhere, Lester made his winning challenge, with Hopeful Venture and Moore eventually gaining second place.

This was Charles Engelhard's second St Leger as he had previously been successful in 1964 with Indiana, who was trained by Jack Watts at Newmarket and ridden by Jimmy Lindley.

Ribocco, whose sire was Ribot and Libra his dam, was certainly a character. If you study the form closely you wonder why there were not a couple of Stewards' inquiries into his running – if only to provide an official answer for the unfortunate people who backed him when he had an 'off' day. It's worth remembering that while he won the St Leger (worth £42,695) and the Irish Sweeps Derby (£57,590), besides being second in the English Derby, he also finished fifth in the Lingfield Trial, was beaten two lengths in the Dee Stakes at Chester and was fourth in the Craven Stakes at Newmarket. He was also third in the King George VI and Queen Elizabeth Stakes at Ascot. Perhaps the oddest race was the March Stakes at Goodwood, worth £1,165, when he was third, six lengths behind the winner, Dart Board. When Ribocco won the St Leger, Dart Board was well behind him, and there had been a remarkable difference of eight lengths. As one of the outstanding racing writers in the game, Richard Baerlein of *The Guardian* and *Observer* fame, remarked at the time: 'Money speaks all languages. Money said Royal Palace would not run in the St Leger. Money said Ribocco would reverse the Goodwood placings with Dart Board.

'Money was right on both counts. No wonder the first advice given to a young man going into racing has always been "Follow the money". It almost seems that Ribocco takes the Racing Calendar to bed with him.'

Ribocco was a lucky break for Piggott. Johnson Houghton, whose training of the horse was extremely skilful, did not have a retained jockey, and so Piggott was ideally placed. And, in a year when Moore and Murless won virtually all the big prizes, Lester was still able to count the Irish Sweeps Derby and the St Leger among his achievements in 1967 – both races which lesser jockeys would only hope to win once in a lifetime.

Ribocco finished seventh of nine in the Washington International at Laurel Park in America in November. The honours in the race went to Fort Macey, an 8–1 shot who beat odds-on favourite Damascus by a nose. Damascus, the

3–5 favourite, seemed to have the race in the bag until Fort Macey stormed through. The winning owner was like the St Leger winner, a man we were to hear a great deal more of, wealthy Virginian Paul Mellon.

Shortly after the Laurel race it was announced from America that Ribocco had been retired and sent to Buckland Farm in Virginia for stud purposes. Charles Engelhard retained half an interest in him and, in January, 1968, he was visited by four European mares, Cursorial, Romp Home, Tanetta and Alzara.

Lester has obviously ridden better horses than Ribocco, but few have been more vital to him at a particular stage of his career than this game little character. He gave Piggott the rides in Classics and near Classics which he wanted. Murless and Moore had a golden time with Royal Palace in the Guineas and Derby, but Lester was not to be outdone.

All season he had travelled hundreds of miles to get any ride he could in his quest to be a champion freelance. The competition from Breasley and Hutchinson could not have been fiercer. When Lester eventually finished with 117 victories it was a winning score and he ended up six in front of 'Hutchie' and eight ahead of 'Scobie'.

In the last few days of the season Lester was prepared to travel anywhere to get on a horse which had chances. And such was his brilliance as he scented another title that he also won on horses which appeared to have no chance. This was the hallmark of an outstanding jockey.

In that first season as a freelance Lester had 100 seconds and 64 thirds. He had proved that his break with Murless was not a rash move. As a freelance Lester was starting a whole new trend in racing. Stables were prepared to engage him while their retained jockeys just had to watch. It created much bad feeling in the early days. But owners and trainers wanted Piggott more than any other jockey in the world. His record spoke for itself and other jockeys just had to accept the situation, no matter how annoying it was for them. One thing was certain – Lester didn't mind upsetting the odd person here and there on his never-ending march to greatness.

By the latter part of 1967 Lester was scoring on several top two-year-olds. He rode Captain Marcos Lemos's Petingo to victory in the Middle Park Stakes over six furlongs at Newmarket. It would have been a bit of a shock if he had not won that particular day as he started at 4–1 on. Then there was Jackie Astor's Remand in the Royal Lodge Stakes at Ascot for trainer Dick Hern at 13–8. And Lester had a good guide to the form of the potential Classic fillies when he partnered the Vincent O'Brien-trained filly Lalibela to victory in Newmarket's six-furlong Cheveley Stakes, which had produced Guineas winner Fleet the previous year.

For the first time in his life Piggott was facing the big decisions which were later to be part of his everyday life – which horse shall I ride in this particular race? More than one trainer wanted Lester for the leading races. In the past he had been with a top stable and all the mounts had been provided. Now he had the choice, and usually whichever one he went for was supported with a mountain of money by the general public.

Lester had changed from the master jockey to the superstar whose selection of rides was just as important as what he did on the racecourse. Predictably, he made few mistakes. He discounted stories of a feud with George Moore by saying: 'It's ridiculous to talk of a feud between us. I regard him as a good rider with that coolness to keep his mounts tucked behind before releasing them for a late run.'

Lester's cousin, Bill Rickaby, wasn't quite such a Moore fan. In his book he wrote: 'For my money Moore was not one of the great jockeys, for while I never saw him lose a race he should have won, I never saw him pull one out of the fire as Lester so often has done. That is the hallmark of a super jockey, being able to win good races on moderate horses.'

For Piggott, the freelance champion, and Moore, Derby victor and winner of many other top prizes, 1967 seemed an ideal year. Both men had started new walks of life and had appeared to have made a success of it. But for one of these jockeys there were vicious background rumblings which hinted of sinister gangsters and big gambling syndicates.

George Moore became the victim of a savage racecourse mob, who terrorized his family to such an extent that he was forced to pack up the greatest job racing could offer. He and his family received many threats. His car was damaged and he returned to his home one evening to find all his clothes had been slashed to pieces. For many weeks, the police kept these stories quiet in the hope that they would apprehend the gangsters. But they had no success, and eventually the story broke of Moore's secret agony and he told Noel Murless that he would be returning to Australia.

The full story of the Capone-type threats on Moore will never be known. It is certain that the impish-faced little Aussie did score many fine victories in England while all this was going on. It's to his great credit that his riding ability in this remarkable year never suffered because of the agony he and his family were having to go through. There are many theories as to why these gangsters selected Moore as their target – many are wild guesses. It is most likely that a group of big gambling men started this campaign to terrorize Moore out of English racing. It's well known that jockeys are not allowed to bet. The Jockey Club are correctly very strict on this point. But it's equally certain that occasionally a jockey must fancy one of his horses to the point that he wants somebody else to put a bet on for him. Clearly, any jockey giving somebody the instructions to have a bet is a clear-cut tip in itself. It seems that George Moore was contacted by some gamblers, possibly from his native Australia, who wanted to operate this system with Moore, especially as he was enjoying such a good season. You only need the courage to have big bets on even-money certainties to end up extremely wealthy. Moore refused to be involved in this type of set-up and the most likely explanation for the attacks was that the gang were trying to terrorize him into playing ball. Again Moore can take credit for the fact that he wanted no part of this, realizing that the

Jockey Club are astute at discovering things about the game which people who are breaking the rules learn to their cost. It's a sad reflection of modern society that the mystery of the attacks on Moore was allowed to go unsolved. And an even greater shame that Moore was so upset by these horrible incidents that he decided to leave England.

Looking back, it's quite remarkable that a man with the Murless job and with such success behind him should have been forced to take this action. From the punter's point of view he had been a daily bonanza. One favourite after another had won for him. But, anyway, Moore decided to go and the Warren Place job was vacant again. If Piggott thought that Murless was prepared to let bygones be bygones he was way out. Murless now turned from an experienced Australian to a Scottish teenager, Sandy Barclay.

In the winter of 1967 Piggott must have happily reflected on his first year as a freelance. He could look forward to more Classic success in the New Year. His father-in-law considered that Petingo was a real flying machine and would be Piggott's main ride for 1968. But Piggott had a sneaking feeling that he had ridden another wonder horse to follow Crepello. Instead of thinking about the two-year-old in the nearby St Gatien stables, he was wondering how a colt in Vincent O'Brien's Tipperary stables was wintering. Lester had fallen in love with Sir Ivor and one of the finest chapters in the Lester legend was just around the corner.

CHAPTER ELEVEN

Sir Ivor wins – and loses

Royal jockey Harry Carr summed up racing's general feeling about Lester Piggott going freelance when he stated: 'I don't think any of the other lads could do what Lester is about to do and get away with it. He can because everybody wants him to ride for them – in England, Ireland and France. He will have to have all the form books at his fingertips and be a damned good picker.'

In 1968 Piggott proved that he could pick 'em correctly, even after only a couple of races on a horse. His obsessive determination was coupled with the rare ability among jockeys to be able to select the better of two horses which appeared likely to run a dead-heat if they ever raced against each other. Piggott had the flair for weighing up the two horses' chances to within an ounce.

The outstanding two-year-olds of 1967 were Petingo and Sir Ivor. Both were unbeaten, both were real speedsters who had obvious Classic chances. Lester had not been troubled when winning twice on Petingo. Equally, he had been extremely impressed by the way Sir Ivor had won the Grand Criterium at Longchamp in the autumn of 1967. Now he was faced with a big decision. Both camps were crying out for Piggott to ride for them. It did look as though one or other of the horses would win the 2,000 Guineas at Newmarket and then go on for the Derby at Epsom. Lester had not made a decision, but one man had already made up his mind very firmly as to who was going to be in the winner's enclosure after the next year's Derby.

Raymond Guest, the U.S. Ambassador to the Republic of

Ireland, owned Sir Ivor and rated him a world-beater. Before the Grand Criterium he backed his judgement with hard cash . . . £500 each way Sir Ivor for the Derby at 100–1. William Hill was the man who laid the bet and stood to lose £62,500.

Before the English season of 1968 got under way Lester Piggott flew to Ireland. He said: 'My object in flying over was threefold. Firstly, to attend the start of the Flat season there. Secondly, I wanted to have my first ride on Blue-rullah, whom I was due to ride in the Lincoln, and thirdly, I wanted to meet Vincent O'Brien to discuss the possibility of riding Sir Ivor in the 2,000 Guineas and then the Derby at Epsom.

'It was not easy making the choice but I finally decided to throw in my lot with Sir Ivor.' It was a historic choice. To people in racing who knew Lester well, Piggott's message for Newmarket was simple: 'Sir Ivor will eat up Petingo,' he said.

Years later Jimmy Lindley told me: 'This was yet another example of the talent of the man. There wasn't a jockey in the country who would not have loved to have ridden either of these horses. On the book they seemed dead level, but Lester knew in his mind which was the better horse and was yet again 100 per cent correct.'

'The first time I got on Sir Ivor,' says Lester, 'I realized that this was a super horse. The feel was similar to that which I got when I first rode Crepello.'

Lester's hopes of winning his first Lincoln on Bluerullah, which would also have been Ireland's first win in this pipe-opener to the season, were dashed when the glory at Doncaster went to Frankincense ridden by Greville Starkey at 100–8.

By the middle of May racing was divided as to whether Lester had made the right choice. But the 2,000 Guineas proved that Piggott had backed another winner and Irish wizard trainer Vincent O'Brien was on the way to repeating the success he had achieved in 1962 with Larkspur, who won the Derby with Neville Sellwood in the saddle at 22–1. Raymond Guest also owned this Classic winner.

At Newmarket Sir Ivor was backed down to 11–8 favourite. In Ireland he was heavily supported and the big bookmakers had to lay the horse for a lot of money for a Guineas-Derby double. It was certainly not mug money. Anybody who was at Newmarket for the Sir Ivor race will have been lucky enough to see the rare Piggott look of happiness. He actually smiled when he came back and when Vincent O'Brien asked him: 'Were you pleased?' Lester said, 'Yes.' O'Brien said, 'Very pleased?' and Lester proved that he really is a man of few words when he answered, 'Yes, very pleased.'

That was the full conversation between two men on the verge of Derby glory. But it was enough for those of us who had seen the way Sir Ivor had won that day. O'Brien raised doubts about the colt getting the extra trip at Epsom. It was the only thing between Sir Ivor and the Derby, many thought. The time of Sir Ivor – 1 min 39·26 secs – was the fastest for four years. Piggott was completely vindicated for making the decision to ride Sir Ivor as it was Petingo who finished second, one and a half lengths behind the then hot ante-post Derby favourite. So Blessed looked well that day and I wondered whether the inexperienced Connaught might turn up a surprise in the young hands of Sandy Barclay, now enjoying his first full season as Noel Murless's top jockey. So Blessed and Petingo were battling it out when they came to the Bushes, Joe Mercer on Petingo seemed to be getting the better of the duel when Sir Ivor and the peerless Piggott suddenly surged into the picture. Anyone who was there that day will hardly forget the sight of Piggott nursing Sir Ivor with a fabulous run on the rail. Petingo made a gallant attempt, but was simply outclassed. By the time Sir Ivor went into the Dip the race was over. It was a classic display by both jockey and horse. Hill's and Ladbroke's took a similar view and quickly installed Raymond Guest's raider as even-money favourite for the Derby.

Between the Guineas and the Derby the experts really had a talking point on their hands. Trainer Vincent O'Brien only lightly touched on the issue when he expressed concern as to whether Sir Ivor would get the trip. The way Sir Ivor won at headquarters convinced me that he would win the Derby by virtue of his outstanding finish. But breeding experts, men in racing who often stand with winning tickets in their hands while less educated people can only tear theirs up in despair, had big doubts. They pointed out that Sir Ivor's pedigree did not give one encouragement. His sire, Sir Gaylord, won over all distances up to nine furlongs in America and he, in turn, was by the miler Turn-To, who was a son of Royal Charger, another miler. She was by the Mahmoud horse, Mr Trouble, and out of Athenia, who was Hyperion's half-brother Pharamond II out of Salaminia. All in all it looked as though Sir Ivor would struggle to get the Derby distance on breeding. But it was hard to forget the way Sir Ivor had won in France and then in the 2,000. Piggott made the correct choice and I, for one, could not forget that betting slip Raymond Guest proudly held. Sir Ivor had cost 42,000 dollars after being bought at the Keeneland Yearling Sales.

At the 40th Annual Derby Lunch at the Press Club in London Charlie Smirke confidently forecast, 'Sir Ivor will make it a walkover.' But Eph Smith told me that he did not think Sir Ivor would get the trip. Many people went for Remand, the second favourite, who was owned by J. J. Astor, whose father, Lord Astor of Hever, had five seconds but never a Derby winner.

I will never forget the day Sir Ivor won the Derby, and not just because of my own financial gain which was large and pleasurable. No, I enjoyed it so much because I thought it was a privilege to be among the huge crowds there that day to see a super horse, superbly ridden and trained, win the world's greatest Classic. And for me it will always be the genius of Piggott which won the day.

I was standing next to an Irishman who had backed Sir Ivor way back in September. His bookmaker had already cancelled his annual trip to Tenerife because he suddenly realized that this raider from Tipperary was going to do the trick. My Irish friend began to sweat up as the parade out on to the Epsom course started. It was a brilliantly hot day and the hip flask in my friend's pocket went in and out like a conjuror's prop. In the stands, packed with racegoers from all over the world, but with the noble Irish race to the front, it was like an oven. But as the runners finished their parade and made their way across the course to the start I focused my glasses on Sir Ivor and Piggott. Here I saw greatness. The magnificent Sir Ivor calmly walking to the start and the ice-cool Piggott gazing around him easily as if he was out on an early morning gallop at Newmarket instead of taking part in such a Classic event with millions of TV viewers and punters willing him to win. The noise of the crowd and the colourful chaos of the people enjoying themselves out on the Downs didn't seem to inhabit the same world as Piggott. His was a more sombre attitude, like a man making his way up the centre aisle of a deserted cathedral.

'He did it in a few strides', was Piggott's explanation for one of the finest Derby displays for years and a victory which clearly put Raymond Guest's hero in the same class as Sea Bird II. They both had that blinding speed which made their rivals look like carthorses when they clicked into top gear.

Blinkered Benroy was the first to show, but when the pace settled it was the impressive Connaught who took over the lead with young Sandy Barclay aboard. Piggott rode to perfection and, as always, in the last eight, Jim Joel's famous red and black colours used by Royal Palace's partner the year before could be clearly seen as the field came round Tattenham Corner. Connaught and Barclay were clearly in front with Society, Atopolis, Laureate, Remand and Sir Ivor in hot pursuit. Then Connaught opened up a clear lead and Remand was obviously not going to reproduce his Chester form which made him such a fancied runner. It was only one and a half furlongs from home that Piggott asked Sir Ivor to put in his best challenge. In those last 300 yards the picture changed completely and Connaught and Barclay were helpless as Sir Ivor stole the show. It was brilliant. If Piggott had been a little cheeky in the Guineas he showed even more last second judgement at Epsom. Sir Ivor's head was only in front for the last 100 yards and he had a length and a half to spare at the end. The time was 2 min 37·73 secs and the eventual starting price was 5–4 on, the first odds-on favourite for many a day. The last odds-on victor was Cicero at 11–4 on, back in 1905.

When I interviewed Barclay after the race he recounted in his Scottish accent how he had thought he had won the Derby at the tender age of 19 – that is, until Sir Ivor came on the scene. He said: 'It was just our misfortune that Connaught was foaled in the same year as Sir Ivor. I really thought that I must win when we were just a furlong from home. When Lester Piggott and Sir Ivor came up alongside us it was as though they had just jumped in.'

Perhaps one's sporting memories will always include gallant losers, the unlucky runners-up. Connaught and Barclay fall into this class. And when Barclay says that he got back to the weighing room and had a quiet tear to himself you can hardly blame him.

Sadly, Raymond Guest was not present to see his chocolate and pale blue colours roar into the lead to land this tremendous gamble for him. He was away in Ireland on official business at the unveiling of the Kennedy Memorial.

Hill's and Ladbroke's were really sick after Sir Ivor's victory. Well over one million pounds was paid out to punters who were only too pleased to cash in on the O'Brien-Piggott roundabout.

Bill Rickaby recalls an incident the very next day after the Sir Ivor triumph. He says: 'When I walked into the weighing room Lester was waiting for me. Before I had the chance to congratulate him on his outstanding piece of riding the previous day, he said: "Are you taking that job in Hong Kong?" When I replied that I had accepted the post of stipendiary Steward to the Jockey Club out there he replied: "You'll be selling your house then. Can I have first refusal?" That was all. No mention of the Derby and no mention of my big decision to go abroad.'

After Sir Ivor's victory many experts hailed Piggott's display as his greatest. Against a field with quite a few top-class performers he had sneaked a win on a horse who was not really a one-and-a-half-mile specialist. In winning his fourth Derby, Piggott had proved that, for my money and many other people's as well, it was hard to believe that there had ever been a better jockey in the world. And that wasn't just money talking. This win took Sir Ivor's winnings to £118,000, and he was expected to become the first horse since Bahram in 1935 to complete the Triple Crown of 2,000 Guineas, English Derby and St Leger.

But first Sir Ivor was due to run in the Irish Sweeps Derby at the Curragh in late June. It was obviously Raymond Guest's hope that he could see his three-year-old colt score an impressive victory in the country where, because of his job, he had permanently moved. It was to be a fruitless mission and one of the most dramatic change-rounds in sport was going to take place.

A 'gentleman's agreement between Vincent O'Brien and leading jockey Liam Ward provided that all O'Brien's horses in Ireland would be ridden by Ward. So when Sir Ivor went down to the start at the Curragh before a massive crowd it was Ward who was seated in the English Derby winner's saddle and Lester Piggott had switched rides to Ribero, whose full brother Ribocco won the Irish Derby and St Leger the previous year. Few of us who watched Piggott canter down to the start at the Curragh that day could have thought that he would beat the 3–1 on favourite Sir Ivor.

There was a slight delay at the start, but eventually the runners got off level. Piggott put Ribero into third position in the early stages and Sir Ivor was last with Liam Ward looking confident. As the leaders turned for home Ward placed Sir Ivor nearer the front runners, Ribero and Giolla Mear. It seemed that he only had to produce half the burst of speed that he had shown at Epsom and he was a certainty. But suddenly it became obvious to the Irish crowd, who had turned out in their thousands to see one of their home-trained champions in action, that when Sir Ivor ranged up to Ribero it was Piggott who held the upper hand. Ribero kept pulling out that little bit extra and there was nothing that

The boy wonder . . . Lester at the start of his career.

One master talks to another . . . Sir Gordon Richards chats with Lester at the special Savoy Hotel dinner in 1954 to celebrate retirement.

A special moment for Lester in January 1960, as he announces his engagement to Susan Armstrong, daughter of the well-known Newmarket trainer Sam Armstrong.

Lester enjoys a spot of golf during one of his trips to Australia.

Lester drives Sir Ivor home in the Washington International at Laurel Park in 1968. British racegoers thought it a great triumph but the American press slated Piggott for the manner of his victory.

A happy racing treble. Trainer Vincent O'Brien (left), owner Raymond Guest and a mud-spattered Lester enjoy the moment of victory after Sir Ivor's Washington International win.

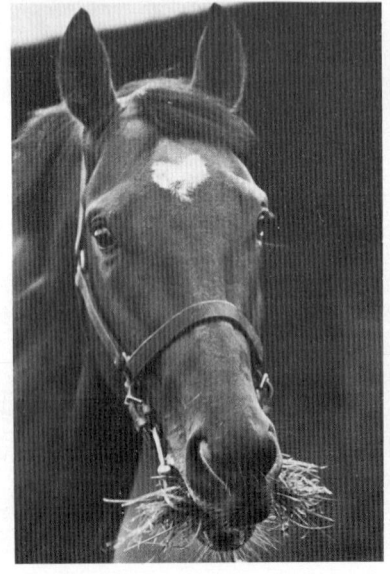

Lester partners Ribero, who gave him the greatest shock of his career when he beat Sir Ivor in the Irish Sweeps Derby at the Curragh in 1968.

Wonder horse Nijinsky at his stables at Cashel in Tipperary.

The moment Lester loves. Here he returns to a cheering crowd after his 1970 Derby win on Nijinsky, one of his finest ever displays.

Lester looks pensive as he waits at the start of the Champion Stakes at Newmarket in 1970 for Nijinsky's final race. Note the lather on Nijinsky which clearly shows that he was not himself that day.

Lester's one-time classic hope, Crowned Prince, at Newmarket when he won the Dewhurst Stakes over seven furlongs.

The Minstrel takes Lester to his eighth Derby win.

It's not often Lester smiles. Here, he leans against the rails at Goodwood after falling off his mount.

Always prepared to spare a minute or two for a young admirer, Lester signs an autograph for an obvious fan.

'A face like a well-kept grave.' This outstanding picture shows the lines on Lester's face which betray years of wasting to keep his weight down.

Ward could produce. It was the real example of the fallen idol. I can remember standing by the winner's enclosure at the Curragh, where there was a general buzz of conversation. Eventually Sir Ivor was led into the runner-up position. Liam Ward and Vincent O'Brien looked as though they were at a funeral. Few words were exchanged and it was obvious that the result was a big shock to the pair of them. Not far away Piggott dismounted from Ribero after winning his third Irish Sweeps Derby in four years. Trainer Johnson Houghton told me: 'I am very surprised. I did not expect him to beat Sir Ivor. He has improved enormously and the sky's the limit now. He will certainly go for the St Leger.'

Liam Ward said: 'Sir Ivor just died in my hands a furlong and a half out and found absolutely nothing.' Two years later on a visit to Ireland I visited Ward at his home just outside Dublin and we discussed the Sir Ivor shock. He thinks that the Derby victory in England possibly took more out of the horse than people imagined. At the time of the Curragh race Sir Ivor was clearly not at his best, although he did improve greatly afterwards and went on to give two outstanding displays.

Lester Piggott will never claim that it was his super riding which accounted for Sir Ivor's downfall. But there is no doubt that once he realized that he had the Derby winner on the run Liam Ward was made to pay heavily for any lack of strength his ride may have had. Piggott said: 'I was placed behind the leaders all the way and two furlongs out when I took a glance at Sir Ivor I thought I was looking at the winner. I was surprised that my horse went on so well and won so easily. The pace was slower than at Epsom.'

Immediately critics found all kinds of faults with Sir Ivor. I think Ward had the answer when he said that the horse was tired after the trip to England and just ran pounds below his weight. Perhaps a measure of Ribero's shock 100–6 victory was the fact that owner Charles Engelhard was not at the Curragh. He was on holiday in Canada.

The odd thing about the form in the Derby was that in the King George VI Stakes at Royal Ascot, Connaught had made mincemeat of Ribero, while Sir Ivor had beaten Connaught with ease at Epsom. But it is worth remembering that the stock of Ribot, sire of Ribocco and Ribero, do make a sudden improvement in the middle of their three-year-old careers. Usually they are not at their best until they have run several races and autumn has nearly started. Still, the race in which Sir Ivor, so soon after his great triumph at Epsom, was dismissed by Ribero will go down in racing as one of the most astonishing change-rounds of all time. It's hard on Ward to state that he had anything to do with the unexpected odds-on defeat. But, at the same time, it's equally certain that Piggott was the ideal rider to cause the upset. Like a boxer who senses that he has his opponent on the run, Lester stepped up his challenge. The result was the shock of the year and caused the saddest and most surprised faces seen at the Curragh, the real home of Irish racing, for many a year.

Perhaps one of the finest clashes seen on the English racetracks for several years came just one week after Sir Ivor's shock defeat. Trainer Vincent O'Brien was never really able to account for his Derby winner's poor display at the Curragh. When the three-year-old returned to the green-carpeted surrounds of Cashel in the heart of Tipperary there seemed nothing wrong with him. O'Brien, never a man to shirk a challenge, agreed that Sir Ivor would run in the Eclipse Stakes at Sandown over 1 mile 2 furlongs the next week. Here Sir Ivor took on the previous year's Derby hero Royal Palace and top French invader Taj Dewan . . . a thrilling contest containing all the class and competition which can draw hundreds through the turnstiles. The big crowd who gathered at the Esher circuit that day were not to be disappointed. Sir Ivor, it can now be claimed, was never happy on the hard ground. When the gilt-edged field turned towards the uphill finish at Sandown he was never able to stride out as well as he had shown at Epsom. Royal Palace, repeating Busted's success of the previous year for Noel Murless, just had the better of Taj Dewan. Here we saw an excellent display of riding by young Sandy Barclay in Jim

Joel's colours. He was on the 9–4 chance and just got the better of the French flier after a hectic struggle. Indeed, many people at the course were convinced that Taj Dewan had won it.

Looking back it's difficult to imagine that within a space of three years Barclay would have been 'sacked' by Murless and that Sir Ivor, who was relegated to third place, was still to give two top-class displays that season, including one brilliant victory.

When Sir Ivor returned to O'Brien's stables the decision was made that he clearly needed a rest. He had been coaxed to a wonderful success in the English Derby and had subsequently been runner-up and then third in races one would have expected him to win on the display he gave at Epsom. O'Brien waited patiently, which is part of his unique make-up that stamps him out as one of the best trainers the racing game has ever known. O'Brien wisely allowed Sir Ivor time to recover and it was to pay handsome dividends.

By now the freelance with the magic flair was being contacted by almost every other trainer in the country. If Piggott did have an almost unfriendly nature which made it difficult for him to foster friendships, it did not alter the fact that astute trainers were only too keen to cash in on his riding powers, which put him on a level higher than any of his rivals.

With Sir Ivor out of the St Leger running, Piggott switched back to his shock Irish Derby winner Ribero. At Doncaster the night before the big race the weather was as wicked as could be. Workers hurried home in a thunderstorm and on the day of the race there was a steady downpour. It was far from ideal conditions for the St Leger, which was first run in 1776, and is over the Doncaster distance of 1 mile, 6 furlongs and 132 yards. It was as wet as wet could be. But not even the weather could take away from Lester Piggott one of the greatest races of his life. If the Sir Ivor job had been done to perfection at Epsom, the way Ribero was short-headed to victory in the St Leger was a masterful exhibition of Lester at his best. All his abilities which make him the best of the jockeys were there that day for the racing world to see.

The heavy going affected the chances of the almost gross Connaught. Noel Murless stated that the rain had damaged any chance Connaught had of success. And Noel should know all about this race. He saddled Ridge Wood to win in 1949 and had a double success in 1960 and '61 with St Paddy and Aurelius, both ridden by Piggott.

Ribero was Lester's fourth Leger triumph. It was the slowest Leger of the century – 3 min 19·8 secs – but Piggott was superb. Ribero was gamely challenged by Bill Williamson and Canterbury in the final furlong. Looking from the stands it seemed that Ribero had just managed to keep off Williamson's typically determined challenge. But the truth of the matter was that for the last 100 yards of the intriguing race Piggott had battled away on a weary horse.

After the race, David McCall, Charles Engelhard's racing manager, said: 'It is fantastic that any jockey could stay so cool. Ribero died in Lester's hands after one and three-quarter miles but he somehow managed to keep him going for the extra 100 yards.' The victory meant, of course, that Engelhard and his then 28-year-old trainer Fulke Johnson Houghton had won both the Irish Derby and St Leger with two full brothers by Ribot out of the British mare Libra in successive years.

It had been Noel Murless's Scipio who jumped out of the starting stalls ahead of Cold Storage and Alignment. On turn there was a dramatic moment when Mount Athos, the Arundel-trained horse who had run so well in the English Derby, was pulled up. Ron Hutchinson did so as he thought that his mount had broken down. Connaught and Sandy Barclay made a brave move but it was obvious that the favourite was hating the conditions. It was equally obvious that only the hard-working Australian Bill Williamson and Canterbury stood between Piggott and more big-race glory. Ribero just held on, thanks to Piggott, to beat the Irish colt with Cold Storage six lengths away third and Alignment fourth. Many people will claim that this was Lester's finest hour. They point out that anybody can win on the best horse in the race. Few men can rival Lester and claim that they won a St Leger by sheer wizardry. The fact that the race was nearly a quarter of a minute slower than Engelhard's two previous winners, Indiana and Ribocco, could not steal any of the praise that Lester so richly deserved.

Piggott was well on the way to his sixth championship in 1968 with 139 winners from 580 rides. He was proving that he could be unattached to any one yard, study the form book with an almost fanatical approach, and still come out on top of his rivals. And not only was he picking up the day-to-day winners with his usual zest, but he was also not missing out on many of the big-race bonanzas.

After the St Leger, as the evenings began to draw in and the autumn months started, it was clear that Sir Ivor was set for a head-on clash with Vaguely Noble, who was owned by a £42,000 syndicate headed by Hollywood beauty surgeon Dr Robert Franklyn. Long before the race, Raymond Guest was challenged to take Sir Ivor to Longchamp for the Arc de Triomphe. Bookmakers quickly installed Vaguely Noble and Sir Ivor as the joint 5–2 favourites in their ante-post book. In their eyes and to the rest of the racing world, despite other top-class runners, this was the two-horse race of all time.

For Vincent O'Brien this was the money-spinning chance to repeat the success of 1958 when Scobie Breasley had ridden King George VI and Queen Elizabeth Stakes-winner Ballymoss to victory at 4–1. But this time there was to be no glory for O'Brien, but the honours did go to another Australian jockey, Bill Williamson. Lester Piggott made a challenge on Sir Ivor, but it was Vaguely Noble, at the English odds of 5–2, who scored for his outstanding French trainer Etienne Pollet, who had produced so many top-class winners from his Chantilly stables, including the magnificent Sea Bird II, Right Royal, Hula Dancer and Never Too Late. Sea Bird II had, in fact, won the Arc in 1965.

When people discuss the races which Lester has boobed

in, it is likely that they will recall the Sir Ivor race in France. It could be true that, once again, the wide straight at Longchamp, banked on one side by the screaming, middle-class Frenchmen and on the other by the fabulous stands and French society, was the scene of a Piggott error. From the panoramic stands, among the best in the world, it is easy to find fault in Lester's Arc finishes.

Yet again Lester had the pick of the top two-year-olds in their leading races at the end of the season. There were certainly no complaints when he nursed Ribofilio to victory in the Dewhurst Stakes at Newmarket at 11–8 on. Bookmakers moved in smartly and named Charles Engelhard's £41,000 buy as the ante-post 2,000 Guineas and Derby favourite. After the success in previous years of Ribocco and Ribero it was hardly surprising. Perhaps it's true to say that there's a dud apple in every basket, but we'll come to that.

Lester also won the Jockey Club Stakes on Riboccare, but it was in the Cesarewitch at Newmarket over 2 miles and 2 furlongs that he really hit the headlines. The Cesarewitch, a long-distance, end-of-season test first run in 1839, had been a jinx race for Piggott and he had never won it . . . that was until October 5th, 1968.

A mountain of money made Major Rose start 9–1 favourite. After he had won by one and a half lengths from Promotion Year, Ladbroke's told me: 'This was one of the biggest Cesarewitch gambles for years. There will be a big pay-out and we have one single winning bet of £10,000.'

I'll never forget the sight of trainer Ryan Price standing in his usual position at Newmarket on the grassy spot just in front of the winning post. When the runners turned into the straight Piggott was clearly visible in the leading group. When he went to the front some way from home, Price darted down to the rails in anger. It seemed that Lester had disobeyed the Captain's riding orders and anybody within earshot of the trilby-topped Findon maestro knew all about it.

But Major Rose and Piggott were in control and the big gamble was landed without too much heartbeating from the punters. Promotion Year and little David Best were runners-up with Teddy Lambton training third and fourth in Lone Wolf and Miss Jack. Actually, Lambton was expected to do better with his third runner, Phil Bull's wonderful servant Philoctetes.

Afterwards Price confessed to me: 'I really thought that Lester had come to the front too soon. But that's why he is such a brilliant jockey. He knew he had the measure of the field and just slipped them in a few strides. Major Rose is all heart and the most genuine of stayers.

'I would have won the race last year with Major Rose, but I admit that I gave Doug Smith the wrong orders. I had not bargained that there would be such a slow pace in the early part of the race.

'This year Lester went to the front because he told me the horse was going so well.' Afterwards poker-faced Lester admitted: 'I was pretty confident that Major Rose would win. He stayed on splendidly.'

This was Ryan Price's third Cesarewitch success. He had also saddled Utrillo (100–8 in 1963) and Persian Lancer (100–7 in 1966). Price told me that he thought the greatest training achievement of his life was Persian Lancer in the Cesarewitch. When I visited him at Findon it was with justifiable pride that he walked out on to the Downs and whistled three horses over to us who had been out in the open. They quickly trotted up to the fence where Price explained that they were Persian Lancer, his Grand National winner Kilmore and 'an old hack'.

Persian Lancer will go down for Ryan as his best training feat, but for those of us who plunged in and 'bet like men' on Major Rose we may be forgiven naming the latter with more financial happiness. Lester showed yet again that when a jockey is needed to produce that little something extra for the big race he has no equals.

Sir Ivor made one more visit to England to run the 1 mile and 2 furlongs Champion Stakes at Newmarket. This race had been the graveyard of many big hopes, but Sir Ivor produced a rare turn of speed and, in O'Brien's opinion, possibly the best race of his career. He gained revenge over French colt Taj Dewan and reversed the placings of the Eclipse Stakes where the French horse had beaten him for second place behind Royal Palace. It was Taj Dewan who made the early running at Newmarket with Lester and Sir Ivor happy to wait some lengths behind. At the Bushes, Taj Dewan began to weaken and from that point, as the mighty Piggott stormed to the front with the minimum of effort, it was obvious that the party was over for all except Raymond Guest's star. Sir Ivor cruised away with the race and it was Locris who trailed in second with Candy Cane third. Sir Ivor had well and truly walloped his rivals.

Only one more chapter was to be written in Sir Ivor's magic year – but what a finale. Sir Ivor and Lester Piggott won the 1 mile and 4 furlongs Washington International at Laurel Park and sparked off one of the most bitter Press battles known in racing. In a thrilling finish, Sir Ivor just pipped Czar Alexander by three-quarters of a length with the previous year's winner, Fort Macey, owned by Paul Mellon, a nose away third. Anyone who had come to support Sir Ivor left with their blood pressure having taken a hammering. It was Ireland's first success in the race and, yet again, it was the sheer genius of Lester which won the day. Second favourite Czar Alexander was quickly away and as the race settled it was clear that Lester was trying to get on to the rails but could not do so. When the field reached the final bend with three furlongs to go, Piggott and Sir Ivor were last. It was here that Piggott made his challenge but found that he could not see daylight. In a split second he switched to the outside to come alongside the leaders. In the last hundred yards Sir Ivor reproduced that blistering burst that wrecked so many hopes at Epsom and it was always certain that Piggott would win, despite the two strong challenges he had to deal with. Laurel Park erupted – with happy Englishmen saluting another display of wizardry from their hero rider, Irishmen cheering home their winner, and the Yanks having, for the first time, to see Piggott steal the glory. And they didn't like it one bit. 'He came far too late', was the general opinion of the American Press, who savagely slammed Lester for his riding. Piggott had won the race with a brilliant use of final-furlong tactics. But he was hounded by the Americans and their words of criticism are something that I am sure Piggott will always resent.

Later he found refuge in the friendliness of the English and Irish Press and said: 'I had little trouble getting through really. The patchy softness in places meant that he kept drifting away from me. I thought he would do it easier than he did. I think he would have won by 100 yards if the ground had not been so soft.'

Vincent O'Brien, his face summing up his joy, such a far cry from the almost unbelieving saddened face that I had seen at the Curragh, said: 'Once he got the opening it was "ping" and that was that.'

A measure of the greatness of Sir Ivor's win was that La Lagune, the highly impressive Oaks winner at Epsom earlier that season, had finished fifth. It was odd that Sir Ivor was bred in Kentucky and trained in Ireland and the second horse, Czar Alexander, was bred in Ireland and trained in America. It was a fitting victory for Raymond Guest, who had quit his post as United States ambassador to Ireland.

For Piggott I think that the success was totally marred by the unfair attacks on him. In racing there's only one pay-out counter and that's for the winner. Piggott had landed the £41,000 prize at odds of nearly 2–1 and the fact that he had only three-quarters of a length to spare was not important. He had won and that was enough. For the Americans to slam him was perhaps rather predictable – and treacherous. I thought at the time that Lester would now put a repeat Washington International win high on his list. We should have all realized that with such an extra drive provided by these comments Piggott would not wait long for his revenge. Twelve months were all this genius needed.

Sir Ivor was obviously voted 'Horse of the Year' and it came as a relief to anguished bookmakers in November when Raymond Guest and O'Brien decided that the great horse should be retired. In 13 races he had won £175,000 for his likeable owner. There was also the £62,500 bet that Mr Guest won and, in fact, bookmakers estimated that the horse won British punters over £3 million. Mr Guest, of course, missed the Epsom Derby triumph and he would have missed the Washington win but for resigning his post in Ireland so that he could back Hubert Humphrey for the American Presidential election. It was the only loser Raymond backed all year.

Early in 1970 there was a virtual tug-of-war to keep Sir Ivor, Europe's most valuable animal, in Ireland. After the Washington success, Guest announced that he intended to let Sir Ivor stay in Ireland as a measure of his thanks for the kindness he had received over there. Sir Ivor, who had cost Raymond Guest only £17,000, became the highest-priced stallion in Britain and, in February, 1970, sired a filly-foal at the Ballygoran Stud. The foal was out of Mr Guest's American-bred County Fleet mare Satanetta.

Sir Ivor. The very name conjures up hundreds of happy memories. From Ireland, where he first ran, to Italy where O'Brien sent him to winter, to England, France and America, he had proved a smash hit. Innocently, most of us thought that the year of Sir Ivor would never be equalled by Lester Piggott. This was the pinnacle of his fabulous career. We should have suspected that there were greater moments to come. The year of Sir Ivor was over. But for Lester the legend went galloping on and already events were taking place on the other side of the Atlantic which were to end up being even more remarkable and sensational than the greatness of Sir Ivor.

CHAPTER TWELVE

Ribofilio – every bookmaker's favourite

When Lester gazes through the scrapbook kept for him by his wife Susan at their Newmarket home he must remember the year of 1969 with immense pride and also terrible frustration. For this was the year of Ribofilio, the speedy two-year-old who won the Dewhurst at Newmarket like a train. But as a three-year-old he became a mystery horse, and while puzzled punters splashed out one losing bet on him after another it was only the bookmakers who regarded Ribofilio with any delight. For them it was the biggest carnival of all time.

Four times he was made favourite for Classics – four times he failed miserably to justify his promise or his price. Mention the horse's name to the bookmaking fraternity and a gentle smile turns into a broad grin as they picture sunny holidays and giant-sized cigars provided from Charles Engelhard's disappointing customer.

For me Ribofilio will always be the Sonny Liston of the Turf. At the start of his career Liston looked a gigantic figure in the field. One thought that only a lunatic would fancy his chances against him. His record seemed to be ideal. At the height of his career it seemed that nobody would ever beat him. But he crashed to the ground so quickly when it did happen that it will always be something of a major sporting mystery. It was like that with Ribofilio and Lester Piggott in 1969. They seemed to have the Classic world at their feet. The Piggott legend seemed to have a near-certain helper to keep the fantastic success story galloping along. But, somehow, everything went wrong.

The golden chance never came along and like Liston it just wasn't a case of near defeat – it was staggeringly wide. It's easy to say that Ribofilio was just not up to the class of Ribocco and Ribero. That's too simple. In all Ribofilio's races there was an air of doubt about the defeat. No, I think when Lester thumbs through that scrapbook he will himself wonder why Ribofilio did not produce even a shade of what was so often expected of him. There must have been frustration for Lester because of this horse. Whether it's because he is missing out on the huge financial rewards or just the glory of winning the big races he hates to be one of the 'also rans'.

Ribofilio kept Lester out of the limelight for a long time. Perhaps if he had switched to one of several other mounts that he could have snapped up he would have kept up his remarkable success in the Classics. Instead he had to wait until there was a bite in the wind and the trees had shed their leaves in November before he really hit the high spots. But I think that the wait was well worth it. In one sudden moment he kept the British flag flying high at the Washington International and made dozens of American Pressmen curse their previous words. I don't know which gave Piggott more personal enjoyment but I have a shrewd idea.

April at Newmarket is the focal point of the world's big hopes for the Classics. Jimmy Lindley, who has had his share of success in big races, told me: 'When you have a runner in the Guineas you are filled with grand ideas. Perhaps the general public don't realize all the hard work that has gone into the preparation and planning of a Classic candidate. The Guineas is where the dreams are either smashed or built on. In this way it is even more interesting than the Derby. At Epsom you have a fair idea what is going to happen. At Newmarket all the hours of planning can be wrecked in a few minutes.'

Ribofilio, a really red-hot favourite at 15–8 after his two-year-old form, was everybody's idea of another Piggott winner. But instead of massacring the remainder of the field Ribofilio trailed in last of the 13 runners. It was a total and sensational failure. For the first time in 1969 – and certainly not the last – the bookmakers breathed a sigh of financial relief.

Watching Piggott return after the race, it was one of the few occasions when the champion showed his bitter disappointment. Whether it's win or lose Piggott is well known for his lack of facial expression. That day it was clear as he spoke to bewildered trainer F. Johnson Houghton after the race that he was a very surprised fellow.

Shaking his head, Piggott said: 'He seems to be all right now. I just don't know what went wrong in the race.' As the racing Press stood in near disbelief the Ladbroke's representative announced that his firm had decided in London to remove Ribofilio from the Derby ante-post list.

Minutes after the race, and amid great confusion, the stewards announced that they had held an inquiry and issued an official statement which read: 'The stewards have enquired into the running of Ribofilio. They interviewed L. Piggott, the rider, and F. Johnson Houghton, the trainer, who were unable to offer any explanation for his poor showing. The stewards ordered a test on the horse to be taken.'

While Ribofilio became the major talking-point that day the fine victory of the Epsom-trained Right Tack from John Sutcliffe's stables at 15–2 almost went unnoticed. Hundreds of watchers at Newmarket and many more on television had only had eyes for Piggott. It was a sad sight as they saw Ribofilio trail in last.

Geoff Lewis rode a typically fine race on Right Tack, who beat Tower Walk (8–1) by two and a half lengths. Noel Murless's Welsh Pageant (13–2) was a head away third with 50–1 outsider Murrayfield fourth. Ribofilio was always tucked in at the rear of the field and with three furlongs to go Piggott virtually pulled him up. In one of the most dramatic sporting moments I have witnessed the Ribofilio hopes for the Classics took a real hammer-blow. Like Liston, the moment of defeat was as surprising as it was embarrassing.

On the morning of the Guineas, Johnson Houghton reported that Ribofilio had appeared absolutely fit and full of life. But while he was usually lively before a race this time at Newmarket he was listless and docile. Piggott deepened the mystery when he recalled that the Guineas favourite had been sluggish and lacked zest on the way to the post. 'From leaving the stall he could not raise a gallop,' said the champion.

Eventually it was reported that the Jockey Club's test had revealed that Ribofilio had not been doped. The test had proved negative. Now the fun really started. Rumours spread that Piggott even went so far as to say that he pulled the horse up because he was afraid that the colt would have fallen down. Never in racing had there been such a terrific turnround in the space of a few days. Before the Guineas, Ribofilio had been ante-post favourite for the Derby. French colt Yelapa had been second favourite for the Epsom Classic, but had finished lame at Newmarket and trainer Maurice Zilber said that he did not think it was at all likely that the colt would run. Ribofilio ran so badly that the bookmakers were entitled to withdraw him from the Derby lists. Only brainless punters would have backed him after the Newmarket spectacle. But it's odd that in three Classics later that summer the general public were prepared to side with Ribofilio to such an extent that he started favourite. I think the fact that Lester showed his loyalty to the colt swayed many people's opinion. They gambled on Piggott's reading of the situation to help fill their wallets. Sadly, for once, Lester tied his genius to a fallen star.

Bookmakers were as mystified by the race as anybody. Now they were faced with making a Derby ante-post book in one of the weakest markets in years. 'If I had a donkey and trained him well for Epsom he'd win this year's Derby,' one seasoned trainer told me happily. After the race it was Caliban, the Noel Murless-trained three-year-old, who became the Derby ante-post favourite. But a measure of his form was that he was sixth in the Guineas and never in a real position to strike. Later it was Hill Run who was installed as the 12–1 favourite. But this was one of the most shaky markets for years.

Right Tack was Geoff Lewis' first English Classic success. The previous autumn they had won the Imperial Stakes and the Middle Park Stakes, but on the book it was Ribofilio who should have streaked away to win from Taffy Thomas' determined challenge on Tower Walk.

Thankfully, the Ribofilio affair benefited from the fact that the stable concerned was so open and the owner, Charles Engelhard, so keen to see that the public did not burn their fingers. After much speculation, Ribofilio finally made a public appearance at Sandown towards the end of May for a trial gallop. At Newmarket it had looked as though he was so bad that one could never see the possibility of him ever racing in the Derby. But he impressed his connections enough to take his chance at Epsom – and, yet again, the punters dived in with their cash. Looking back it seems amazing that he could ever have started favourite to win the world's finest race after the dismal Newmarket flop. It shows just how short the memories are of punters and how much esteem they put on the selection of Piggott for a race.

When a hot favourite gets beaten in a big race it's usually the poor bookmakers who carry the slanderous can. At Newmarket it was a fact that Ribofilio's price did drift out to 5–2. The racing correspondent of *The Times*, Michael Phillips, had bravely pointed out: 'Somehow everybody in the ring seemed to know that Ribofilio would not win.' It was an opinion which was quickly questioned but an interesting one. Of course, the negative result of the test showed that no old-fashioned nobbling had been done with evil-minded bookmakers behind some sinister plot. Thanks to the way racing is run that kind of thing does not exist these days. At times like this, guesswork is the order of the day and men's reputations can be carved up at a fast rate of knots. The bookmaking industry was whispered to have been behind this business. It was a foolish argument, not even worthy of a whisper.

On a personal note I would point out that after the Guineas, I, too, had opted for guesswork and had formed the opinion that Charles Engelhard's colt would never be at the post for the start of the Derby. I just could not believe that the horse would win the race and I guessed that he would not start. This being the case I offered a friend of mine 50–1 against Ribofilio winning the Derby, odds he was happy to accept with £2. I was still convinced that Piggott would not win this particular Derby as I arrived at Epsom for the big race. I had seen Blakeney finish second in the Lingfield Derby Trial and thought that this was good enough form in a bad year to take the big prize. But I had the rather unpleasant experience of standing next to the late bookmaker, Victor Chandler, and seeing Ribofilio backed down to 7–2 favourite for the Derby with a deluge of money. When you have offered 50–1 against a horse it's a rather un-nerving experience to see the general public back the same animal down to 7–2. That's bad enough, but when you have Lester Piggott to beat as well it's not the ideal recipe for a Derby trip. Luckily, for me, Ribofilio finished fifth, but there was a tense moment when the horse did look as though it was going to make a determined challenge. Blakeney was the hero of the day at 15–2 and proved a real triumph for trainer Arthur Budgett, who not only trained the colt but bred him as well and had a half-share in him.

When Arthur Budgett announced that he had engaged youngster Ernie Johnson to ride Blakeney in the Derby he raised quite a few eyebrows. Many people thought that an inexperienced rider who had never ridden in the Derby before was hardly the ideal partner for a Classic contender. But Johnson gave a masterful display – especially for one so young. And yet again it was the magic of Lester Piggott which in no small way contributed to the success of Johnson. The night before the race Johnson had gone to Budgett's Berkshire home to watch films of Piggott winning his four Derbys. It was a lesson of greatness and some of the Lester skill obviously rubbed off on Johnson as he won the race so coolly, using virtually the same route as the far more

112

experienced master Scobie Breasley had used on Charlottown three years previously. At one point I can recall wondering whether Johnson would get through the small gap which was left to him. But, riding in a style which suggested that he had won a dozen Derbys before, he just managed to squeeze past Shoemaker and Brian Taylor. Ironically, Peter Walwyn, who had a succession of big-race seconds, had thought that his Stoned was his best Derby hope and stable jockey Duncan Keith had the ride. He finished eleventh, but Shoemaker did eventually come second to Blakeney at 25–1.

Ribofilio was still made ante-post favourite for the Irish Sweeps Derby with Blakeney his chief rival in the market. Yet again the British public plunged in and it's little wonder that when bookmakers gather together in a huddle and discuss their Horse of the Century, it's Ribofilio who wins by a distance. It was Christmas Day every day as punters – and not all of them were mugs – sided again with this amazing horse.

Before leaving the Blakeney Derby, it should, of course, be mentioned that French jockey Jean Deforge became an absolute villain of the piece as far as people who had supported Prince Regent, who finished third at 13–2, were concerned. He lay back in running and played a waiting game. But with so many mediocre runners in the race he was asking for trouble – and that's certainly what he got. Deforge was not the first top-class jockey to find Epsom a curving mixture of twists, turns and frustration. When I visited likeable Irish Jockey Liam Ward at his Ashleigh Stud a few miles out of Dublin he once joked to me: 'Epsom? It's a terrible racecourse. It should have been blown up years ago.' Deforge, who finished by far the fastest on Prince Regent in the Derby, would surely have seconded Ward's motion about Epsom.

But thanks to the Lester films and a cool head it was Johnson who stole the glory. I always liked the story he told me about his journey to the crowded Surrey course. 'Just as I was driving into the car park,' said Ernie, 'I noticed a small boy who kept tapping on my window. Eventually I pulled the window down and he handed me one of those plastic red roses. I said I didn't want it but he forced it into my hand and I thought to keep him happy I'd have to have it. Then, suddenly, the kid's mother emerged from behind a car and snapped, "Five bob, please, dear." I paid up and kept the rose in my car. Perhaps it brought me luck and I kept it in the car after winning the Derby until the damned thing faded away.'

Johnson was caught for a mug by one of the many smart tricks used to diddle the public on such occasions. But once the Derby started Johnson was nobody's fool and his victory by one length was greeted by several happy punters and all the bookmakers. For once Piggott had not sent a cold shiver down their spines with another big Derby pay-out. This time the tables were reversed and Ribofilio was the toast of the day as they lit up their giant cigars.

When the 15 runners lined up for the start of the valuable Irish Sweeps Derby at the Curragh on June 28th there was one significant change. Instead of Jean Deforge in the saddle on Prince Regent it was the cheerful countenance of Geoff Lewis aboard. At Epsom Geoff had ridden 18–1-shot Agricultore and the colt had certainly caught many an eye in the paddock with his good looks. But looks are never everything as somebody once said, and Agricultore never really promised to give Geoff a win at his local track. In fact, they had finished 19th. But now Lewis was on Prince Regent and any criticism of Deforge was certainly more justified as the new combination swept to victory. Runner-up was Ribofilio. In a bad year for Lester as far as the Classics were concerned this was probably the colt's best display and it was only in the last 100 yards that the French-trained runner stole the prize.

Prince Regent was last to leave the stalls as Ballantine set off at a brisk pace. When Ballantine dropped back it was Onandaga and Reindeer who zoomed to the front, closely pursued by Ribofilio and Blakeney. At one crucial stage it looked as though the vast sums of money invested on

Ribofilio were, at long last, going to show a dividend as he hit the front. But after going past Reindeer it was Lewis who produced a blazing burst on the Etienne Pollet three-year-old to win by a length. Ribofilio was second with Reindeer, owned by Raymond Guest, third and Blakeney a short head away fourth. Prince Regent was owned by Comtesse de la Valdene, the sister of Raymond Guest. It gave Geoff Lewis the Irish Classic double as he had previously won the 2,000 Guineas on Right Tack for John Sutcliffe's Epsom stable. Said Geoff: 'I tracked Ribofilio and waited until almost the last half-furlong before showing my hand. I was very confident as I knew that Prince Regent had a fine turn of foot. When I asked for the big effort he just lengthened his stride and that was that.'

Lester offered no excuses. 'Prince Regent was too good for me at the end,' he said sadly, no doubt cursing the fact that the £53,410 prize had been pipped from under his nose. In big races in recent years it has too often been the case that top jockeys have been blamed for the defeat of fancied horses. It seems to be the immediate reaction to the defeat of a leading horse in the betting market. I think that on several occasions the jockeys have been unfairly slammed.

After the Irish Sweeps it was claimed in some less-informed quarters that Piggott had been caught napping. Nothing could have been further from the truth. He had ridden a perfect race and had been pipped by a better animal. Prince Regent's victory did not point to any lapse on the part of Piggott, who nearly always produces a copy-book finish in big races.

The finger of guilt, clearly shown by Geoff Lewis' handling of Prince Regent, must surely point to Jean Deforge. If Prince Regent had been ridden in similar style at Epsom he must surely have won the English Derby. At the Curragh, Blakeney was well beaten, although Ernie Johnson did say after the Irish race: 'Blakeney was never the same horse that won in England. He was never happy and niggled a lot. Long before the end of the race I knew that we were not going to win.'

So ended another race with Ribofilio not in the winner's enclosure. This time it was Prince Regent at 7–2 who proved the winner. The million green smackers which were won by the bookies in 1969 on Ribofilio were to make the horse one of the most valuable losers of all time ... to the bookmakers.

But Lester, who rode 163 winners that year for his sixth successive title, was not always giving the turf accountants a winning summer. If he had not broken his contract with Noel Murless and taken the successful role of a freelance he would probably have won the Eclipse Stakes on Royal Palace the previous year.

Ribofilio actually did Lester his greatest favour by getting the cough. Early in July he was found to have the cough and was withdrawn from the Eclipse. Piggott was booked to ride Ribofilio, and so had no ride. Henry Cecil, who became son-in-law to Noel Murless, and quickly showed that his future as a Newmarket trainer was rosy, was only too pleased to engage Lester to ride the five-year-old Wolver Hollow. But it did not seem that Wolver Hollow had much chance against that outstanding mare, Park Top, trained also at Newmarket by Bernard van Cutsem for the Duke of Devonshire. Park Top had been ridden twice that year by Lester and was a warm favourite to add the £30,000 to her win kitty. Instead it was a typically powerful finish on 8–1 Wolver Hollow by Lester which floored Park Top and Geoff Lewis. So Ribofilio's coughing outburst indirectly handed Piggott a £2,000 pay-out for riding the winner. The owner was 101-year-old American Mrs Hope Goddard Iselin, who was having her last runner in England.

It was perhaps typical of the way Lady Luck can smile on you in racing. In Ireland Lewis just pipped Piggott. At Sandown it was the champion who had the glory. Years later I asked Lewis about the race. With his usual honesty which makes him such an outstanding jockey and personality he told me: 'Yes, I did ride a bad race that day. But in the life of a jockey you are bound to ride a stinker. And with the public following you every day it's only reasonable that you must accept the criticism.'

By late July racing's amazing wheel of fortune had spun again, and not for the first time by any means the trump cards were dealt to Piggott when he now rode Park Top in the £31,122 King George VI and Queen Elizabeth Stakes at Ascot over 1 mile and 4 furlongs. If the St Leger won on Ribocco was a gem and the Sir Ivor Derby victory another sparkling show, this was one of the glittering moments in Lester's never-ending chapters of greatness. At one stage Park Top was way behind the others. People who had made Park Top the 9–4 favourite may have been biting their nails in anxiety, but Piggott was at his brilliant best. Great jockeys are men who have an outstanding sense of pace and tactics. They can plan a finish from a mile out, taking into account all the other runners in one glance. That day Lester showed what we all knew he had, the unique flair to do the right things at the right time and make it look so easy. From the stands it looked a simple destruction job of the rest of the classy field. In reality it was superb horsemanship and jockey-manship – two different things – at their highest.

It was Chicago's pacemaker, Coolroy, who was soon in front. Timmy My Boy, Hogarth, Symboli and Crozier followed in a second group. When the field entered the straight it was clear that Piggott's mastermind had told him in a flash that a daring route up the inside by the rail was the way to wreck his rivals' chances. In the Eclipse Stakes at Sandown, Geoff Lewis twice tried to find a suitable opening for Park Top. It cost the mare the race as Piggott pounced. Now it was Piggott who got to work and his line of attack to the winning post was as straight as an arrow. He slipped Park Top into the lead a furlong out and then gave his supporters that moment of confidence when he cheekily gazed across at Crozier, who battled on for second place, and Hogarth, who finished third for jockey Ferrari.

Fifteen years before, Piggott's career had been in shreds after his suspension following the King Edward VII sensation on the same course. Now Lester had shown all the trade marks of a great jockey as he completed a hat-trick of King George VI victories. Lady Luck had again smiled on Lester and Park Top – but they did not capture her attention for the whole summer and in early October that wheel of fortune had spun in a different direction. In the then £90,000 Arc de Triomphe at Longchamp, Lester again had to be content with second place – again to Bill Williamson, who in the space of two years twice picked up £20,000 for three minutes' work. This is the race where a jockey can make a small fortune quicker than a maid can make a cup of tea. After his success with Vaguely Noble, Williamson completed a brilliant double on the Seamus McGrath-trained Levmoss, which was also owned by the trainer from Cabinteely, just outside Dublin.

But the day still belonged to the fabulous champion jockey from England as he completed a breathtaking four-timer which won more than £68,000 for four lucky owners in one afternoon. Yet it was the race he didn't win which upset Lester. He claimed: 'It was my own fault. I left my chance too late. I should have won.'

The late trainer Bernard van Cutsem was a great Piggott admirer. But he once told me: 'Jockeys in the class of Lester Piggott are extremely rare. I'm inclined to think that when they do make a mistake it's usually a rather bad one.'

While most Pressmen and racing experts will agree that Lester did, perhaps, ask the mare to do too much I find it interesting that Peter Scott, Hotspur of the *Daily Telegraph*, and one of the most respected writers on the sport, thinks differently. He has family connections who supervised the breeding of the remarkable Park Top. Peter told me: 'I just won't have it that Lester made a mistake on Park Top. The mare had to be ridden in a certain way and Lester always used the same tactics. I don't blame him for the defeat at all. Levmoss was a very much underrated horse. Only the race before the Arc de Triomphe he had been given a huge weight to carry in a handicap at the Curragh and had absolutely trotted up.'

Of Park Top, Lester says: 'She was a great mare. Great character. She knew what she was supposed to do and did it. She goes into the gate as if she was going into church and comes out as if hell were after her. She knows more about racing than I do.' Such words of praise from Lester – particularly the last sentence – must make Park Top one of the best of them all.

I'm afraid we certainly can't say the same about Ribofilio. His fourth upset had come in the St Leger. Here he was backed down to 11–10 favourite as punters tried to back this colt on the one time he clicked. They should have known better. It was good money after bad and only men with enough faith and fivers to fill the vaults of the Bank of England plunged in.

This time it was 7–1-shot Intermezzo and Ron Hutchinson who pipped Ribofilio and Piggott into second place with Sandy Barclay on Prince Consort third. The distances of one and a half lengths and two lengths represented yet another swoop for the bookmakers. As the Harry Wragg-trained three-year-old stormed over the line it was said that Piggott should have made his challenge sooner. Cries of 'Good old Lester' were not the order of the day at Doncaster, but perhaps it was the last time that the public backed Ribofilio thinking that he was an exceptional animal.

In racing history he will go down as one of the most expensive flops of all time. It was at Newbury on October 25th that the final chapter in the Ribofilio book of boobs was finally written. The 100,000 dollar colt gave by far and away the worst display of his career in the St Simon Stakes. Yet again he was the chief market fancy, but he trailed in more than 25 lengths behind the Noel Murless-trained Rangong, who snatched a last-stride win from Torpid. The fact that he didn't start at 33–1 that day just shows what mugs punters can be at times.

In November Charles Engelhard decided to try Ribofilio on American racecourses before sending him to stud. Bookmakers cried into their champagne. Beaten favourite for four Classics, well over a million pounds had changed hands that summer – in one direction. His two-year-old form when he won the Chesham Stakes, Champagne Stakes and Dewhurst Stakes stamped him out as an outstanding customer. But, from the moment he flopped in the Guineas behind Right Tack, his career might as well have been over.

One of racing's great mysteries will always be what went wrong with Ribofilio that day at Newmarket? Whatever it was, we will probably never know. All we do know is that the colt was never a winner afterwards from Epsom to the Curragh, to Doncaster, to Longchamp for the Arc de Triomphe and finally to Newbury. It was a tale and journey of woe. The fact that so much money was gambled on this colt, who at one stage looked set to join racing's immortals, is in no small way a credit to Lester Piggott. Even though on form he had no chance in most of the races he ran in as a three-year-old he was still heavily punted on. The one fact that L. Piggott was in the saddle was enough to make hundreds of people stand in a queue to back him. But he never produced the goods like Ribocco and Ribero had done before him.

Mention of Gerry Oldham's Intermezzo reminds me of a previous race in which he had finished in front – only to be disqualified and placed fourth. In the 1969 Great Voltiguer Stakes over 1 mile and 4 furlongs at York, which will always remain one of my favourite racecourses, the race was awarded to 4–6 favourite Harmony Hall, who was ridden by Bill Williamson.

The previous year Lester Piggott had produced a major shock by finishing first on Ribocarre. But Sandy Barclay and Connaught, the 1–3 favourite, were awarded the race by the stewards. Lester's cousin, Bill Rickaby was on Scipio, Connaught's pacemaker in the race, and says: 'Lester and Sandy had one or two brushes in my last season and I know that the champion was furious when the stewards disqualified him on Ribocarre and awarded the race to Sandy and Connaught. I was surprised that the stewards awarded the race to Sandy, even though the two horses came very close together in a driving finish.

'Sandy should have had the race sewn up without any trouble and he would have won easily if he had got to work earlier on Connaught, who needed a bit of riding to get the best out of him. That Lester pulled Ribocarre together and got out of him one last fling on the finishing line was typical of this great rider. That he complained afterwards was most unlike him, because I had never before heard him complain to another jockey about a race incident, an objection, or the stewards' decisions.'

That Piggott-Barclay clash was one of quite a few after the young Scotsman had taken over Lester's old job as first jockey to Noel Murless. They objected to each other on various occasions and even somebody who did not know the inside secrets of racing could tell that there was something of a minor feud between them. 'I have nothing but the greatest regard for Lester,' said Barclay at the time. But the compliment did not tell half the story.

Champion for the sixth time, Lester was a happy man as he started to relax a little towards the end of the season, although there was no framed picture of Ribofilio hanging from any wall in his home. Yet again he had ended top of the chart and also had a fair idea of the two-year-old talent which would the following year carry his Classic hopes. In a moment of rare impetuosity, Lester had named the French-trained Breton as his probable Epsom Derby partner after they had produced a thrilling burst of speed to win the Great Criterium at Longchamp over one mile at 22–10. Among the others who had trailed in behind that day were Baroque, a length away, and the much thought of Gyr. The richest juvenile event in Europe had produced another superstar for Lester to think about.

Breton, a brown colt by Derby winner Relko out of the Chanteur II mare La Melba, had won the Prix de la Salamandre at Longchamp over seven furlongs. Until that time it was thought that Amber Rama was the pick of the French youngsters, but in the Salamandre Breton reversed an earlier defeat. It was thought that Gyr, who did not have the best of runs in the Criterium, would go for the Prix du Jockey Club at Chantilly and that Mick Bartholomew might persuade Lester to ride Breton in the English Derby.

These thoughts were probably in Lester's mind as he flew out to America in November. He had two targets on this mission and was determined to make sure that they were both achieved. Mission number one was to do everything in his power to repeat his previous year's Washington International success on Sir Ivor by winning on the Bernard van Cutsem-trained Karabas. Mission number two was to prove to the American Press that he was not as they had labelled him after Sir Ivor's win – a 'bum' jockey. Piggott had been deeply hurt by the taunts of the Press the year before and was itching to make them eat their words.

The Times racing correspondent, Michael Phillips, must surely be forgiven for getting sentimental about the 1969 Laurel race when he observed that the ideal quotation for Piggott and Karabas after their quite splendid victory was Rupert Brooke's words: 'If I should die, think only this of me: That there's some corner of a foreign field That is for ever England.'

Over 30,000 racegoers packed into the Laurel Stadium expecting the much-fancied American favourite Hawaii and Czar Alexander to battle out the final stages. How wrong they were. In the biggest upset in the U.S.A. since the Red Indians took on General Custer, Karabas and Piggott recorded a one and a quarter length victory that will remain as one of the most treasured moments in the history of British racing. And remembering the words that had been levelled at him the year before, it's a fact that for one of the few times in his career Lester returned with a broad grin on his usually poker face. It tickled him to see the Yanks proved so wrong.

When asked by stable connections before the race what Karabas' chances were, Lester replied: 'There's nothing to worry about now. The turf was my only worry. But I have never known it so good. We'll win all right.'

122

People who were with Lester before the race say that they have never known him so confident. One racegoer from England told me: 'I saw Lester before he had changed for racing and I couldn't believe it. He was joking and talking to friends of his. He seemed very light-hearted and you would not have thought that he was about to ride in one of the most important races of his life. He seemed to know that he was going to show the Americans that he was the super jockey the rest of the world made him out to be.'

Brazilian entry Sabinus caused a rare hold-up at the stalls and eventually had to be backed in from the front, even with blindfolds. Piggott had moved Karabas to the rail by the first bend and when they came to the short straight – it's only about one and a half furlongs, like Chester – it was Hawaii and Czar Alexander who headed the field. But they went wide and Piggott, seizing his chance at the drop of a hat, stormed to the front. In the end he had one and a quarter lengths to spare and one of the greatest victories of his career had been achieved.

Bernard van Cutsem said proudly: 'He was beautifully ridden. The race went as far as I had planned it. He is a good and charming horse.' Lord Iveagh, who owned the horse in partnership with his stepfather, Roy More O'Ferrall, also paid a big compliment to Piggott on the way he had handled the four-year-old. By winning the race twice, Piggott established himself still more as an international rider of the highest order and joined Manuel Yeaza and Jean Deforge as the only men to score two Laurel successes.

Piggott had again proved his supreme ability to ride a patient race. The Americans could not understand why he had ridden Sir Ivor the way he did the previous year. Now with the loud cheers of English racing fans saluting Piggott on his repeat triumph they were beginning to get the gist of his greatness. Lester took exception to his critics the year before and he was for once in his life only too pleased to exchange a few words with the Press – particularly the Americans. Piggott will not be remembered for what he has said in his life. For him, actions have always spoken much louder than words. But his after-race comment to the home Pressmen will surely be one of the few sentences from Lester's lips that will go down in racing history. When asked at what stage he thought he would win the race, Lester calmly replied in his own rather nasal fashion: 'About two weeks ago.' Exit about 30 red-faced U.S.A. scribes.

Lester failed to understand why he had been slammed for his riding of Sir Ivor, who had won the race fair and square. 'Sir Ivor had to be held up for a late burst in order to last a mile and a half in soft ground,' said Lester, who, had to travel thousands of miles before he let his hidden emotions finally hit the surface in that winning smile.

With this victory at 7–2, Piggott registered the one win in the world that meant most to him. It was typical of the restless genius that it should happen only 12 months after the unhappy hour following Sir Ivor's win, when he swore to himself that he would show the Americans the riding magic we all know so well. The writer from across the Atlantic who wrote that Piggott was a 10 lb handicap to Karabas obviously knew as much about racing as a snail. Lester had gone into the enemy's camp and scored a sensational first-round knock-out.

CHAPTER THIRTEEN

A horse called Nijinsky

The tiny two-seater plane which descended from the sky above Ireland's Rock of Cashel, formerly the seat of the ancient Kings of Munster, in March, 1969, brought together the most fabulous combination horse racing will probably ever know. When people talk of the outstanding horses of all time they will talk of Ribot, Sea Bird, Nearco and such magic names. These were the greats. But in days to come, when people talk of Lester Piggott, the champion of champion jockeys in my opinion, they may well talk of Piggott as the man who rode Nijinsky.

Nijinsky. The very name fires with enthusiasm and romance the imagination of any person interested in racing. If the greatest authors of all time had huddled together and tried to write a novel about a horse they could not in any way have captured the magic of Nijinsky or the way he won a million hearts. No rich film producer could create the atmosphere that this creature could instil. This was the wonder horse of all time. He had simply everything. A wonderful owner in Charles Engelhard. A wizard trainer in Vincent O'Brien, and a jockey fit for one of the finest racehorses ever to grace the Turf, Lester Piggott.

The dawn clouds had just lifted above the Tipperary mountains to the back of Vincent O'Brien's gallops, possibly the best in the world, as the Cashel trainer and Piggott walked through the big Georgian house, alongside the white post and rail fence and out on to the gallops. The world of Nijinsky had just started.

Maurice O'Callaghan was Vincent O'Brien's head man at

the time. He had handled all of O'Brien's superstars over the years and had been in Italy when Sir Ivor had wintered there. Looking back to that memorable day when Piggott and Nijinsky came face to face for the first time, Maurice told me: 'Lester arrived around 7.30 and we were told to prepare Nijinsky. They only went for a shortish gallop, but I can recall that O'Brien was really pleased at the end. It seemed that horse and jockey had hit it off first time. Lester seldom spoke to any of the stable lads. But when he returned I looked up at him and asked, "How good is he? Will he win next year's Classics?" Lester simply looked down and snarled, "He'll do . . ." ' Simple words from Piggott which were to come true.

The story of Nijinsky and Lester Piggott is a story that surpasses all other feats of racing greatness. With the advent of television and legalized betting the average man in the street has become far more aware of the Sport of Kings. Communications and wide newspaper coverage have brought into most people's homes the attraction of the Turf. Let's face it, it's the fourth biggest industry in Great Britain.

Nijinsky and Piggott didn't need selling to the public. Whether it was the owner's private fortune which inspired the James Bond character 'Goldfinger', his trainer's record which made his rivals also-rans or his jockey's ghost-like personality and near unbelievable displays in the saddle, Nijinsky was an advertiser's dream. Yes, the Nijinsky and Piggott combination provide a story which contains everything. To a certain extent it's a fairy-tale. But unlike most fairy-tales this one didn't have the happiest of endings. Had it done so perhaps the legend would have been even greater. But it's a story which has the victories, the massive crowd appeal and, at the end, the tragedy of defeat that, perhaps, even the conquerors did not want to see.

With his successes with Ribero and Ribocco – let's not mention Ribofilio – Charles Engelhard was an obvious admirer of the Ribots. When, in the summer of 1968, he heard that a Ribot colt was among some coming up from his Windfields Farm to Toronto for the annual auction he pressed Vincent O'Brien into making the trip across the Atlantic to view the situation. That's the esteem in which Engelhard held O'Brien for his opinion of horseflesh. When Ireland's leading trainer saw the colt he was forced to tell Engelhard that it was not a good purchase as there was malformation of one of the forelegs. So one of Vincent's longest trips looked like being a wasted journey. But life and racing are funny. How many people have discovered magical stars by mistake? It's a long list and the name of the great Nijinsky can be accounted among them. For while Vincent O'Brien was at the auction he spotted a Northern Dancer colt. Within a few hours, Vincent persuaded Engelhard to pay the Canadian record yearling price of 84,000 dollars for Nijinsky. 'He had a wonderful set of limbs, a good head and he appealed to me,' Vincent O'Brien said afterwards.

Towards the latter part of the 1969 season the English racing world was very much aware that Vincent O'Brien had a flying two-year-old. For the first time the name Nijinsky was on everybody's mind as they thought ahead to the following year's Classics.

Nijinsky made his first appearance in the Erne Stakes over six furlongs at the Curragh. He started at 11–4 on and won by half a length. From that race he won the Railway Stakes at 9–4 on with the much-fancied Decies five lengths behind him. Again over six furlongs he won the Anglesey Stakes at the Curragh, this time starting at 9–4 on. And the fourth success came in the Beresford Stakes over a mile at 7–2 on.

Already the Irish countryside around Cashel was whispering the mighty deeds of this tearaway two-year-old. He had already won £8,800 in prize money and slaughtered the best two-year-old company in Ireland. Now the scene was set for his first trip to England and his first race with Lester Piggott.

For the fifth time in his career Nijinsky went to the post the odds-on favourite. This time, with Lester in the saddle, he was 3–1 on to win the Dewhurst Stakes over seven furlongs at Newmarket, the race which Lester had won on the ill-fated Ribofilio the previous year and on Crepello way back in 1956. Nijinsky could not have been more impressive in his three-length victory from Recalled with Sandal three lengths away third. He was held up by Lester at the start and switched to the outside to challenge one and a half furlongs from home. From that point Piggott had it won.

In Richard Baerlein's excellent book entitled *Nijinsky – Triple Crown Winner*, Lester says that he was not really able to gather much from the initial race on Nijinsky's back. 'He didn't have much to beat, but he did it very easily,' was Lester's comment. But Piggott did decide that day that this was to be his Classic horse for 1970, and his previous idea of partnering the French colt Breton was dropped. O'Brien said: 'After the Dewhurst I was confident that Lester would ride him in the Classics. The only doubt from then on was how far he would stay.'

Following the Dewhurst, William Hill, who, strangely, was never a real Nijinsky fan, offered him at 3–1 ante-post for the Guineas and 7–1 for the Derby. These are the prices the O'Brien followers in Ireland were to make their fortune on. Looking back it seems near criminal that we all didn't cash in. Maybe it's that the smart ones among us did so.

The following March the tiny plane again descended on the green-carpeted countryside near O'Brien's Ballydoyle stables. Lester Piggott was again to be reunited with the horse that was to become a household name in 1970 – a real box-office star. Nijinsky made his début that year in the Gladness Stakes over seven furlongs at the Curragh. As in all his races in Ireland he was ridden by Liam Ward, who had a gentleman's agreement that he rode all O'Brien's horses in Ireland. This time Nijinsky came in to 6–4 on and was probably the best value for a bet in his entire career, although for the first time he was taking on horses older than him. Four-year-old Deep Run was second, four lengths behind Nijinsky and Ward.

Now everybody knew that this really was a colt of exceptional class, and when he came to Newmarket for the 2,000 Guineas he was 7–4 on and won in one of the best ways a

Classic hope could ever hope to. I was standing next to Joe Mercer in the stand facing the finishing post at Newmarket that day. Joe had been held up in India for a spot of customs bother and was not riding in the big race. I remember Joe's comment when Piggott and Nijinsky took over the lead about two furlongs from home. I can't reproduce Joe's exact words, but they were to the effect that he was going to walk it. Many people thought that Lester would reproduce the type of blinding finish he got from Sir Ivor to beat his rivals. But Vincent O'Brien was keen that he should not be 'covered up'. Instead he told Lester to let him move through the field and not undergo any sudden acceleration. Piggott rode another perfect race and completely to his trainer's instructions. Because of Nijinsky's breeding it was a widely held theory that he would not get the Derby distance of one and a half miles. Several experts thought that Nijinsky was too much of a speedster to be a genuine stayer of the Epsom distance.

In obeying Vincent O'Brien's instructions that Nijinsky was not to be held up for a late run like Sir Ivor, Lester was not worried when Nijinsky hit the front some way from the line. 'He could have beaten them at any distance, whether it was one furlong or six furlongs. He had terrific speed and that's why we did not really know until after the Derby whether he would stay,' was Lester's summing-up. Nobody could complain about the way Nijinsky had slammed his rivals over the straight mile at Newmarket, but there was concern that he may have been a little idle once he got in front.

The late great William Hill, the most outstanding bookmaker of all time, was a fine student of form and breeding. When other bookmakers were quiet as statues he would go through a field of 25 runners and shout out a price for the lot. He knew racing backwards and it's true to say that one of the major errors of judgement he ever made was about Nijinsky. He was one of the most well-known people who firmly believed that the Irish star was not the type to win the Derby. He was one of the first people to congratulate

Vincent O'Brien in the winner's enclosure at Newmarket, but he also told the trainer that 'There was not a lot of motor left at the end of the race.' Perhaps racing history will show that Nijinsky's 2,000 Guineas display rather split the experts.

The betting for the Guineas showed that in the public's view it was virtually a one-horse race. The bookmakers went 7–4 on Nijinsky and then 13–1 Tamil, 100–7 Amber Rama, Without Fear, 100–6 Yellow God. It was, in fact, the Yves Saint-Martin-partnered Amber Rama who set the early pace. When the runners reached the two-furlong mark, the easy, bobbing style of Bill Williamson could be seen at work on Yellow God, who overtook Amber Rama. It was at this point that Piggott eased Nijinsky on to the scene and when the Irish colt released his final run the race was virtually over. Inside the final furlong Nijinsky lengthened his stride and he finally won by two and a half lengths from Yellow God, who belonged to David 'Mr Racing' Robinson.

Prices from 5–2 down to 7–4 were quickly snapped up by punters with Hill's and Ladbroke's. But there were still many, many people who even after the Guineas did not realize that the Horse of the Century was just a few weeks away from an Epsom triumph. Unbeaten in seven races, Nijinsky had still not convinced everybody that he would be the Derby victor. I suspect that both O'Brien and Piggott had a fair idea, though!

In the winter months they had thought at one stage that it would be Mrs John W. Galbreath's Great Heron who would be the main Classic contender. Sired by Sea Bird, it was always O'Brien's opinion that he would mature a little slower than Nijinsky and it was 1970 rather than the previous year that would be the vital one. Great Heron only won his first race on a disqualification, and he subsequently lost to Decies and slipped down the O'Brien ratings. Lester Piggott had cantered to the front on Great Heron when riding him in the previous year's Observer Gold Cup. Then the Newmarket-trained Approval came with a blistering run and Great Heron could find nothing to match him.

As the days to the Derby disappeared it was Approval

who carried many people's hopes. He had finished a sad fourth in the one and a quarter mile test at Sandown behind Cry Baby, but in Newmarket he was seen as a possible winner. His jockey, Greville Starkey, told me several times before the big race that he would win the Derby on Approval. Young trainer Henry Cecil had certainly made a big impression since getting his licence. The French entry Stintino won the Prix Lupin in Paris prior to the Derby and was soon backed. So, too, was Charlton, who scored a fine win for the Queen at Goodwood.

Meanwhile, Nijinsky returned to O'Brien's stables to be given the final workouts by a man who was about to prove yet again that when it comes to training winners of big prizes he has no – repeat no – rivals. And Lester Piggott went about the work of a champion jockey with his usual determination and drive. Although he was on the verge of a Derby success with thousands of pounds involved on the outcome, he still put as much effort into a seller at Ally Pally. I think that one of the most amazing things about this champion of champions is the way he sets out for each race with the same goal – he wants to be the winner. There is no more gratifying feeling when one has backed one of Lester's rides than to see him come to the front. It's like watching a goal ace like Kevin Keegan heading for the penalty area. You know that a real professional is about his work, every muscle and limb working in harmony to conquer his rivals.

As the Derby drew near it was clear that the bookmakers would lose close on £2 million if Piggott and Nijinsky won the race in which there had originally been 667 entries. But it was equally certain that there would be only one real winner of the race whoever was first past the post. The total bets for the Nijinsky Derby totalled something like £7 million, so the Government with its betting tax was going to get a final rake-off of £400,000. The ante-post boys got a late bonus when the Queen's Charlton and Politico from Noel Murless's stable were both scratched because of injury.

After Nijinsky's final workout in Ireland, Lester Piggott,

who flew over specially for the trial, said: 'I was very pleased with the colt's performance over six furlongs. It was most satisfactory.' Bookmakers' reaction was to reduce Nijinsky to 5–4. The horse the bookies wanted to win was Stintino, but they were going to be mighty disappointed.

With the chance of riding a wonder horse like Nijinsky you would think that the Irish colt would be the only horse on a man's mind with the big day getting near. Not so superman Piggott. He tried to get down even further in his battle against the scales and was taken ill at Newmarket. I saw him that day and I can tell you that it wasn't a pleasant sight. He is not a bad-looking fellow with his close-cropped hair, but that day the expression on his face told that he had gone too far with his dieting. When he went for his usual sip of water between races he was taken ill. I will deal later with the almost unbelievable dieting this man endures, but it's worth noting that even with the Derby so close he was still prepared to make even greater sacrifices. His will-to-win has never stopped for half a second.

Charles Engelhard, like most people connected with racing, was highly superstitious. For a man who was worth over £100 million it seems odd that he should worry about anything – but he did. He had not seen many of Nijinsky's seven wins and even contemplated missing the Epsom race because he was worried that he might change the winning run. But he could not miss the Nijinsky race because, as he said: 'I think that this is the best horse I have ever owned. We will soon know. I wish the race was run in America because I think I would stand a better chance of winning there. Luck would be on our side. I am so nervous when I am at a race that I can hardly bear to watch my horses. I usually hand my binoculars to my manager and I can judge how well the horses are going by looking at his face. If he goes pale . . . I know we have lost.'

Shortly after Engelhard's plane had touched down at Heathrow Airport, a smaller plane reached Gatwick Airport after midnight and the main passenger went into secret quarters. The millionaire who specialized in precious metals and precious horses was about to enjoy the greatest moment of his life that money couldn't really ever buy.

On the day of the 1970 Derby I wrote in the *Sun*: 'Gyr will trot up, claims Brian Taylor. Nijinsky won't be beaten, says Sandy Barclay. Approval will win for England, boasts Greville Starkey . . . that's the view of three ace jockeys. But the entire racing world is certain of one thing about today's Derby – Irish-trained favourite Nijinsky will be ridden by the greatest jockey of all time, Lester Piggott.

'Far away in the lush surroundings of Vincent O'Brien's stables in Tipperary the Irish are mourning the loss of their great chaser Arkle. But they are keeping champagne on ice to celebrate another champion – ridden by a man who can win the fabulous £63,000 Classic as coolly as he lights one of his giant cigars.

'Sandy Barclay, who rides Cry Baby, told me last night, "I followed in Lester's footsteps after he left the Noel Murless stable. It was the biggest step any jockey could take. I have tried to think what Lester would have done had he been on horses I was just beaten on. When I rode Connaught in the 1968 Derby I thought that I had won 100 yards from the post. Then Lester burst past me on Sir Ivor and my dream was shattered. After coming so near to winning the major Classic at the age of 20 I was very upset. I cried afterwards. I think Lester is the greatest and no one on the tracks can match him. Nijinsky has a really outstanding chance tomorrow." '

'Greville Starkey, bidding to win the race for trainer Henry Cecil, disagrees about Nijinsky. But he cannot argue against the Piggott opinion poll. "He is a wonderful fellow and the finest jockey in every way. He's so dedicated. Look at the way he made himself ill trying to lose 2 lb at Newmarket on Saturday. If I had half his money I would not waste so hard. Still, he can have his Nijinsky. I know there is a lot of confidence behind him, but Approval is in peak condition and I am sure he will not be beaten. It's Stintino I fear most and if we do fail in the Derby we'll go for the St Leger."

'Brian Taylor, rated Lester's closest friend among the other jockeys, will be watching from the stands today. He strongly fancied the French-trained Gyr. "I think that Gyr is a brilliant colt and I saw him win his first race in France from an impossible position. If he runs like that again, he'll trot in. He always comes good for the big occasion."

'The last time England's champion jockey and wizard trainer O'Brien teamed up in the Derby was two years ago when there were doubts whether Sir Ivor would stay the trip. But with a brilliant burst inside the final furlong Sir Ivor streaked home. The same question mark hangs over this year's Guineas winner.

' "I don't think he'll stay the trip," says Taylor. "He has the right jockey in the saddle, that's for sure, and if anybody can get him home it's Lester, but I don't think he will win this time. Of course, Lester is the tops. He is so cool and has never been seen under pressure."

'Says Jimmy Lindley, who rides local hope Mon Plaisir, "Smirke was great, so, too, were Elliott and Richards, but Lester is the champion of them all. He never gives up. I came second on Indiana in 1964 and know there is no other race like the Derby. Only in the Derby and the Arc de Triomphe do you really notice the roar of the crowd. When you come to the end of these races and the crowd get excited and start shouting it's like opening an oven door for the jockeys. You can feel the heat of the tension."

'Ron Hutchinson rides The Swell. He tells me, "I must admit that Lester looks very hard to beat. It's only on breeding that there can be any doubt about Nijinsky lasting the mile and a half. It's a serious business the Derby and everybody is tense. You plan how you will ride your mount and who you will track. Then the gate opens and things rarely work out quite as you had hoped.

' "Lester drives himself hard and deserves to be champion. But Geoff Lewis is just the same. He is up before six every morning and travels miles to ride at sometimes two meetings a day. Lester is not the only one who diets like mad. Jimmy Lindley once told me that the only moisture

which goes into his body each day is if he sucks his tooth-
brush."

'So there you have it. The glittering prize that every owner
and trainer dreams of. The undulating Epsom circuit, the
champagne suppers and pickpockets mingling together and
the greatest horseman the world has known.

'That's the Derby 1970.'

June 3rd was the day to remember. As it had been two
years before when Sir Ivor won, it was a sweltering day. The
sun shone brightly and the buzz of excitement in the packed
stands, which resembled the Kop at Liverpool's football
ground, could almost be handled. When there is a real
world-beater in the race and a large section of the nation
have backed him the atmosphere is electric. So it was with
Nijinsky.

In 'Tatts' the bookmakers sweated that Piggott would not
land his fifth Derby. Charles Engelhard joined thousands of
punters in an almost grilled state as they yearned for the
magnificent Nijinsky to do his stuff. Watching the colt's connections in the paddock before the race revealed a never-to-
be forgotten occasion: the picture of Vincent O'Brien,
top-hatted and looking extremely dapper, talking in his rich
Irish brogue to Piggott. Two maestros chatting peacefully. It
could have been that first chat way back the previous March
on the gallops at Ballydoyle after Piggott's initial workout
with Nijinsky. There was no sense of tension about O'Brien
and Piggott. They had seen it all before. Racegoers were
attracted like a magnet to the sight of O'Brien giving Piggott final instructions. These two men had won the world's
top prize before and they went about the pre-race routine
seriously, but not nervously. The general public crowded
round and on television millions of viewers watched Lester
Piggott climb aboard the horse, just as he does every afternoon. Look at his face and you would not have known that
millions of pounds and a racing legend were involved. Piggott went unsmiling and coolly on to the course. Meanwhile
the racing world watched and waited for another display of
the Lester magic.

Nijinsky was soon backed to 6–4 on the course from 11–10. He went back to 6–4 before a late rush sent him back to 11–8. Gyr was the interesting one and as several tipsters had gone for him a flood of money reduced him from 4–1, 7–2 and 100–30. One of the country's top tipsters, Peter O'Sullevan, has a wide knowledge of the French racing scene. Besides being able to pick out 30 closely packed runners on a murky day at any meeting in a few seconds he also knows the French form like Parisians know the way to the Eiffel Tower. Not surprisingly, Peter was a great supporter of Gyr and the *Sun*'s tipster, Lionel Cureton (Templegate), was another expert to doubt whether Nijinsky would get the trip.

Anybody who was at Epsom that memorable day will never forget the Nijinsky victory. For the very first time in his life Nijinsky started at odds against. In the early stages, as the huge crowd hushed to watch and listen to the commentary, Piggott settled Nijinsky into sixth place. As the field came round Tattenham Corner it was 80–1 shot Long Till and Duncan Keith who were ahead, being closely pressed by Meadowville (Geoff Lewis), Cry Baby (Sandy Barclay) and Mon Plaisir (Jimmy Lindley). Piggott had Nijinsky close up and Bill Williamson was also well placed on Gyr. Two and a half furlongs out it was Great Wall (Joe Mercer) and Long Till who disputed it, but it was clear that Gyr was going to be the one they all had to beat. Inside the final furlong, Piggott allowed Nijinsky to quicken and with the crowd roaring 'He's done it', Nijinsky went clear to win by two and a half lengths from the gallant Gyr, who was only headed in the final furlong by the Irish colt. As he had done on Sir Ivor, Piggott held up Nijinsky until the best possible moment and when his mount clicked into top gear there was nobody who could match the finishing speed. Little wonder that Vincent O'Brien, puffing very happily at a relaxing cigarette after the race, said: 'He slammed them. My one doubt about the stamina was knocked for six. Before the race Lester told me, "They will never be able to get us off the bit." I never tested him over his distance. The temptation was there, but I waited until the big day and now he's done it.'

Lester came out of the jockeys' room with the look of a very contented man. He looked more flustered as he dashed off to the Royal Box than he had done on Nijinsky.

'We were always cantering. A grand ride, a great horse,' he told me.

I have two memories of the after-race scene. As I chatted to O'Brien, the more than ample right hand of Noel Murless emerged to shake his Irish counterpart's hand in congratulation. 'Well done,' said Murless. 'This is the greatest horse since Ribot.' That praise from Murless meant a great deal to O'Brien. It was one master praising another master's work and that's not all that common.

As the crowd went mad with delight bookmakers started counting the cost. I don't imagine Ladbroke's chief Cyril Stein had his usual happy and satisfied look that afternoon. William Hill accepted his error in judgment, while it was clear that, yet again, Piggott's opinion had been completely vindicated. Stein actually reported his firm's loss at £50,000. 'Some people deserted Lester at the last minute,' he said.

In the many joyous bars, packed by the rejoicing masses, thousands of hangovers were quickly being created. In the plush boxes the smoked salmon was pushed to one side as the champagne corks popped like gunfire. There's nothing like celebrating greatness – and this was the case with everything connected with Nijinsky.

One would have expected to have found Charles Engelhard's massive frame resting as he sipped some celebration champagne in one of the boxes. Instead, the news-hungry Pressmen found him sitting under one of the stairways as shelter from the boiling heat. He was seated on some empty beer crates and swallowed Coca-Cola out of the can. 'Struggling to get down these stairs was harder work than Lester had,' Engelhard joked as perspiration dropped off his brow. It was the most unusual after-Derby Press conference with a winning owner. Even the most anti-capitalist could not have denied this very human man his hour of glory. Like O'Brien, he said his only worry about the race was that Lester did not hit the front until very near the end. 'But then I looked through my glasses at Lester and could see that he was not moving. I knew then that everything was going to be just fine,' said Engelhard. As he mopped his brow, he looked a far cry from his role of platinum king. He rated Nijinsky's value at £1,250,000 and added: 'I have waited since 1948, when I first watched the race, to win it. It's the No. 1 race in the world.'

This was Piggott's 16th Classic winner in Britain and Engelhard's racing manager, David McCall, said: 'Lester must have been the most confident jockey ever. He must have been, to just sit in fourth place until the final furlong, happily watching his chief rival wing away home.'

One man who backed Nijinsky was politician Lord George Brown. He was making an election tour at the time and thought of a novel way to inspire support. At one meeting he told his listeners that Nijinsky would win the Derby. In the little Norfolk village of North Walsham the inhabitants all followed George's tip. 'The odds are not good,' said George, 'but I'd rather be on a winner than a loser – that's why I'm saying vote Labour as well.'

Nijinsky produced a little bonus for Lord Brown in his popularity poll, but he didn't have a double win. Labour, although favourites like Nijinsky, were pipped in a photo-finish by the Tories. Lord Brown later quit the House of Commons for greater things. The villagers of North Walsham still talk of him kindly, though, and wish he'd pass through there more often just before the Derby.

We know now that O'Brien thought that Nijinsky was a bigger certainty than Sir Ivor. Lester says of the victory: 'When he was cruising in the straight he was not going very well and I had to get stuck into him a bit. This woke him up and he went on to win easily enough. I think I hit him twice. At that time I thought that he was probably better than any horse I had ridden.'

The fact that Nijinsky was only 0·88 second outside Mahmoud's record time of 1936 in the hands of Charlie Smirke confirms what an outstanding display it was. Perhaps it's true that both Connaught and Gyr will go down in history as an unlucky pair. But for the genius of Sir Ivor and Nijinsky – backed by the masterful riding of Piggott – they may well have been good Derby winners.

There were just 24 days between the Epsom race and the Irish Derby which was Nijinsky's next stop. Lester knew that Liam Ward had a gentleman's agreement to ride all O'Brien's horses in Ireland, but that did not stop him from trying to do a deal with Ward to ride the horse at the Curragh. Piggott knew that he had won the Derby on a really outstanding colt and he did not like the idea of anybody else riding him with the juicy thought of the jockey's winning percentage. Ward refused to play ball on any idea to change the agreement, which was quite understandable.

I met Liam Ward and his wife Jackie, the daughter of impresario Jack Hylton, at their stud farm. They are racing's most charming couple. Liam joked with me as he lit up a small cigar: 'The cigars Lester smokes are like my table legs, not like these little things.' He told me of how he had rung up a friend in Ireland and went on to imitate Lester's voice as it was Piggott who answered. The champion happened to be staying there. It was very amusing to hear Ward describe how Lester had told him on the eve of the Irish Sweeps Derby that Ward would win the race. Liam had asked why Lester was bothering to come over in that case. 'I shall be second,' Lester had replied. When Nijinsky and Ward duly picked up the £57,012 first prize at the Curragh, Lester's prediction came true and he was second on Meadowville, three lengths behind. That's typical Lester. If he knows he can't be on the winner, he'll try and move heaven and earth to be second.

After the major upset of Sir Ivor two years before, punters willingly took 10–1 on Meadowville in the hope that Lester was going to do a Ribero on Ward. This time it was

139

different and Nijinsky was in better shape than O'Brien's previous hero. A bogy has often hung menacingly over English Derby winners at the Curragh but not so Nijinsky. He went on superbly to join Santa Claus as the only colt to complete the Derby double. 'Nijinsky first – the rest nowhere.' That was the headline in the papers after the Curragh canter. Ward rode a fine race and waited with Nijinsky until the right time before producing the victory burst. Ward's only worry was the full lather that had broken out on Nijinsky before the race. Michael Kauntze, an Englishman who is O'Brien's assistant, told Ward not to worry as Nijinsky did the same at Epsom. But Ward thinks that he only did this to give the Irishman a little encouragement. Liam told Pressmen after Nijinsky's win at 11–4 on: 'My grandmother would have won on him today.' It was a typically sporting comment from a man who sadly may well be remembered for the race on Sir Ivor that he did not win. The Curragh victory took Nijinsky's winnings to £170,000. What a horse! And what an easy £5,701 for Ward for his 10 per cent of the winnings. No money could have ever been made easier on a racecourse.

After the Irish Sweeps success, Charles Engelhard was quoted in one newspaper as saying: 'I am especially keen that Nijinsky will go to stud with an unbeaten record.' Lady Luck or a rare error by Lester was later to wreck the Engelhard dream, but it's worth recording that the 'unbeaten' tag did mean a great deal to Engelhard, who was obviously aware of Ribot's unblemished history.

'The King George VI Stakes was probably Nijinsky's best race ever because he was up against older horses, but he still won in a canter.' So said Lester Piggott about the King George win. There were only six runners for the £31,993 one and a half mile event, but it lacked nothing in class. The previous year's Derby winner, Blakeney, was in the line-up as was the previous year's French Oaks winner, Crepellana. Add to this Karabas, Lester's Washington International hero, Italian Derby winner Hogarth, and Coronation Cup winner Caliban, and you realize it was no walk-over for

Nijinsky. It was a clear pointer of Nijinsky's greatness that he should go to the post at 85–40 on with a horse like Blakeney at 100–7. It was Blakeney who followed Nijinsky home, but there was never any doubt that Lester would win when he challenged in the final two furlongs after being held up. To win such a gilt-edged event by two lengths was yet another example of this horse's outstanding qualities and how Piggott always got the very best out of him. By winning the King George, Nijinsky topped the £200,000 mark, and in making it ten out of ten galloped past Sir Ivor's previous record of £169,956.

After talk that breeders from Britain, France and Ireland were preparing a £2 million bid to keep Nijinsky in Europe, Nijinsky completed the first Triple Crown since Bahram had done so 35 years before when he won the St Leger at Doncaster over 1 mile, 6 furlongs and 127 yards. It was announced that Nijinsky would never race as a four-year-old and that he would retire to stud in Kentucky.

Nijinsky won the Leger by one length from Meadowville and started a big talking point in racing. Richard Baerlein wrote in the *Observer* after the race: 'Nijinsky won without appearing ever to be called up to get into top gear by his rider, Lester Piggott.' Other experts were not so sure. Nijinsky had suffered from a skin infection and had been plagued with spots. It was the severe attack of ringworm that in O'Brien's opinion caused him to lose 29 lb after the St Leger. Says O'Brien: 'This loss proved that he wasn't as hard and fit as he should have been. The time between the recovery and the Leger was too short. Nevertheless, he had to have a preparation race for the Arc and the Leger looked sub-standard with no weight to give away.'

Having watched the Leger, I was a little worried about Nijinsky's display. For my money he had not shown that little extra sparkle which put him on a par with any horse of the century.

As racegoers dashed back to London the talking point was Nijinsky. Was Piggott sitting so quietly on Nijinsky because he thought he would canter away with the race, or was it because he really had to nurse Nijinsky home ahead of Meadowville? As the points were discussed late into the night by the great army of Nijinsky fans, I don't suppose there was a man alive who would have gambled that Nijinsky would never win another race in his life. But that's the cruel way Charles Engelhard's luck ran out.

Before what was to be the final crowning glory for Nijinsky, the Arc de Triomphe, I flew to Ireland to see the champion in his final preparations. Stay at the famous Queen Anne House, which was formerly the Archbishop's Palace at Cashel, and you enjoy the luxury of this wonderful part of Ireland. Since about A.D. 370, because of the security of the remarkable Rock, Cashel has been the seat of the Kings of Munster. St Patrick was a former visitor to Cashel, which is 100 miles from Dublin in well-farmed, fertile land. Now, with the unbeaten Nijinsky trained a few miles away, the eyes of the racing world were focussed on it.

After driving past the massive Rock of Cashel, which stands out on the skyline in great splendour, it's not hard to realize that Cashel is a horse-mad town. When I visited the town before Nijinsky's Arc de Triomphe race it was clear that everybody was eagerly awaiting the race. They wanted to see the horse retire undefeated, which would not only give 'Your Man' Vincent O'Brien further success, but also give some to Tipperary, the home of the Horse of the Century.

Long into the night I talked to local farmers and broken-down old English lords about the Nijinsky legend and the trainer in a thousand just down the road. As the shorts became longer and the wonderful racing prints on the walls of previous Derby winners seemed to come to life in the flickering candlelight it became obvious that it was not only Charles Engelhard who wanted to see Nijinsky retire with his superb record intact, it was the whole of Cashel.

A few miles from Cashel is the little village of Rose-green, a remarkable place in that it is not only small but has facilities that any major borough would be proud of. See the fine church, swimming pool and other impressive buildings and you wonder where the hard cash has come from to produce these luxuries. But the 200 people of Rosegreen are lucky folk. They live in the same area as a brilliant trainer, who has wealthy owners. Wealthy owners who are prepared to provide gifts for the village to celebrate their victories. Once it was just a crossroads village, now it's well and truly on the map.

Irish millionaire John McShain started the ball rolling in 1957 after Ballymoss won the Irish Derby and the Arc de Triomphe. He dropped £1,000 into the kitty. When another O'Brien horse, Larkspur, won the 1962 Epsom Derby, Raymond Guest gave £1,500 towards the cost of a park. Then, when Mr Guest's Sir Ivor obtained his great success with Lester Piggott, out of the blue came a cheque for £2,000 towards a new school. Charles Engelhard gave the village the 'green light' to build a gymnasium and indoor heated swimming pool after Nijinsky cantered away with the Irish Derby. No, if the inhabitants of Rosegreen had to pay for all the fabulous facilities out of the rates they would all be broke tomorrow. This is the land of O'Brien, of great horses and a great jockey called Lester Piggott.

Vincent O'Brien is not a figure who becomes involved greatly with the locals. His wife plays the organ at Mass on Sundays and he'll give a friendly wave to any of his friends as he zooms past in his expensive motor. But O'Brien's world starts at the notice which says 'Strictly no admittance – private', on a corner of the road just outside Rosegreen. Down at the end of the long drive is Ballydoyle, a white-painted Georgian house which always reminds me of the house in the film classic *Gone with the Wind*. It's peaceful and quiet.

When I visited there to see Nijinsky I almost expected to hear the heavenly choir start up as I approached the house. In the hallway are pictures of some fine horses. Gaze up and down at the colour photographs and it looks like a pictorial history of leading post-war racehorses. Then you study the caption and see the words 'Trained: M. V. O'Brien'.

O'Brien is the best trainer of them all, I am told, because

he spends more time with his horses than any other man. No small detail escapes this master. Here in the middle of this rich pasture land of green grass Nijinsky was trained for his career. Nine times his weight in gold – that was Nijinsky. He was syndicated for a record £2¼ million before the St Leger, so whether he won the Arc de Triomphe did not affect his cash price. Thirty-two people had shares of £72,000 each.

Before the Arc, I visited Bill Williamson at his then home in Oxshott, Surrey. I'll never forget the little Australian they called 'Weary Willie' emerging from behind a massive drinks cabinet with an ample Napoleon brandy. The man who had won the previous two Arcs and had been described by Lester as 'the best jockey in the world' made fascinating listening. Bill told me: 'After Vaguely Noble and Levmoss I'd dearly love to be the first jockey to finish in front of Nijinsky. It's true that Etienne Pollet stayed in training just to handle Gyr as a three-year-old. Gyr didn't like the track at Epsom and I expect him to run much better at Longchamp. I'm not unhopeful that we can beat Nijinsky.'

I also talked to Liam Ward, and he told me with a little sadness in his voice: 'Lester's got the rides now. I know that I will never ride Nijinsky again. But don't get me wrong. It would break my heart if this horse was beaten, no matter who rode him. But I know it will never happen.' Liam's wife, Jackie, remembers the day Liam returned from a trip to O'Brien's stables. She told me: 'I will always remember Liam coming home and saying that, although it was Great Heron whom big things were expected of, it was another horse called Nijinsky who would be the one to follow.'

Sunday, October 2nd, was the Arc de Triomphe – a day that will be recalled by racing people for scores of years. It will be discussed over and over again. Only the one sad aspect of the race, Nijinsky's defeat, remains the same each time. Nijinsky earned £238,716 before the Arc, but it was not so much that final £100,000 prize which mattered but the hope of Engelhard that his farewell would be a winning one to place him firmly in Turf history on a par with or even ahead of Ribot, who, like Kasar, Motrico, Corrida and Tantieme, won two Arcs when he hammered Europe's best horses in 1955 and 1956. The previous year Levmoss had produced a 52–1 shock, but in 1970 it was all the rage that Nijinsky would win the 1 mile, 4 furlongs at Longchamp's palatial stadium.

The race had proved the Waterloo of many Arc contenders and Lester Piggott had not always displayed his greatest skills there. Now Nijinsky was set to end the bogy once and for all. Thousands of British supporters flew over. They arrived in Paris with smiles and jokes galore. By nightfall the airport lounges were full of downhearted supporters – many who thought that Nijinsky and Piggott could never be beaten. The champ had been k.o.'d by a stunning blow.

As Nijinsky and Piggott made their way out on to the Longchamp circuit the fabulous stands were packed with racegoers of all nations. They had one thing in common – not one of them thought Nijinsky would be beaten. As the flags of the European countries involved fluttered high above the stands the setting looked just right for Nijinsky to prove beyond all doubt that he was the Horse of the Century.

In the tree-lined paddock before the race, photographers had crowded round Nijinsky as though he was some glittering film star. The man sitting on the horse took no notice whatsoever. It would have been a big shock if he had been affected by the occasion. Nijinsky was different and the reception he got from the near fanatical crowd that day did nothing to improve his chances.

Nijinsky's twelfth test started with Piggott being drawn on the outside. In the early stages he only had three horses behind him. When the runners swung into the wide straight it was Yves Saint-Martin on Sassafras and the Geoff Lewis-partnered Blakeney who hit the front. When Piggott did make his late run on Nijinsky he quickly drew alongside Sassafras and the result looked like win No. 12 for the Irish runner. Blakeney began to weaken out of it but Sassafras matched Nijinsky in the last strides and driven in great style by Yves Saint-Martin stayed on well as Nijinsky just could not find anything extra at the finish.

When it was announced that Sassafras had won by a head the Engelhard-O'Brien-Piggott dream was over. But they did not need the announcement to tell them the result. As Saint-Martin passed the post on the 19–1 shot he threw his hands into the air in delight in winning his first Arc. For Lester this was the saddest moment of his life. Being second in successive years on Sir Ivor and Park Top was a terrible ordeal. Being beaten on Nijinsky was like hell.

When my memory of this race deserts me I shall still have one sight firmly fixed in my mind – a tragic moment which summed up the terrible disappointment of a man. As Nijinsky was brought back to the paddock where ten minutes earlier every camera was flashing in his face, there was Vincent O'Brien, standing sadly like a broken man. He was near to tears and understandably as he told Pressmen in a soft voice: 'He had a lot to do. I do not want to be critical but his move was a little late.'

Clearly after the race, when impressions are crystal clear, the Irish trainer did think as millions of television viewers had opined in Britain, that Lester had left his challenge too late. The big debate on the Arc defeat of Nijinsky will always hinge on the question: Did Lester boob? According to Richard Baerlein's book on Nijinsky, both O'Brien and Piggott attached a great deal of importance to the high draw. 'I was happy with the race apart from the final two furlongs,' says Lester. 'But the draw meant that I was not able to ride the kind of race I wanted to. He did swerve to the left when I hit him. I suppose he was tired.'

Two things emerge from the race. Clearly Sassafras would never have beaten a fully tuned-up Nijinsky and, secondly, while I accept that the draw was not in Piggott's favour, he still did leave the horse a mammoth task in the straight. The talk of the draw, which was not, I hasten to add, widely aired on the actual day of the race, is not supported by other Arcs. The French filly Pistol Packer was drawn 18 in 1971 and,

146

but for the flying finish of Mill Reef and Geoff Lewis, she would have been the victor.

I prefer to think that the skin infection meant that Nijinsky had run below his top health in the St Leger. He was still far from his high-powered self on the day of the Arc. The draw may have been against him but it must be said that Piggott left him a lot to do.

Perhaps the most honest assessment of the event I've heard comes from Lester's father, Keith Piggott, who met his son shortly after his return to England. Keith says: 'I saw Lester and could see how disappointed he was. I said that I thought he should have won. Lester looked at me knowingly and said, "I know. I had a great chance to go over to the rails at one point in the straight. I could have done it but I was frightened that the French stewards would have done me." That's the fear that haunts Lester in all his races, especially the big ones and in France.'

Perhaps lesser mortals than Lester should never criticize his horsemanship. The outbreak of ringworm probably had a much bigger contribution to the defeat than people imagined. And the photographers who swarmed round the mighty horse, pestering him like a horde of bees, did nothing to help his chances. Only one thing did emerge from the Arc – it probably saddened more people than any other race in the history of the Turf. If Nijinsky had won the Arc he would never have raced again. But both O'Brien and Engelhard thought that they owed it to their hero to let him end his career on a winning note. Nijinsky recovered from the trip to Paris well, although he lost 11 lb on the return trip. Five years later I was relieved when connections thought that Derby hero Grundy, well beaten in the Benson and Hedges at York had done enough, and he went to stud, missing the Champion.

Although Nijinsky started at 11–4 on for the Champion Stakes worth £25,078 it was clear to anybody who watched Nijinsky closely before the race that he would have all his work cut out to beat his eight rivals. Yet again, photographers and the admiring crowd probably did more harm than good. When Nijinsky went out on to the course he was obviously affected by the occasion. He was on edge and for the first time in his career he went down to the post uneasily. A few minutes later, when Nijinsky cruised up to the leaders, it was the old familiar sight. But in the last 100 yards Piggott was not able to inspire Nijinsky and it was Lorenzaccio, ridden by Geoff Lewis, who caused the shock. The Noel Murless-trained five-year-old made every inch of the running. Nijinsky failed by one and a half lengths to win his final battle.

It was another sad sight. Lester Piggott blamed the hero-worshipping crowds for Nijinsky's final defeat. 'There was even a big crowd at the starting gate. He was in a real state by the start of the race and at halfway I did not think that he would be in the first three.'

One of the things I most admire about Lester Piggott is that when he had been beaten for the second time in 13 unlucky days he had the honesty to admit: 'He is still the best horse I have ever ridden.'

For Lester to admit this is, perhaps, the finest tribute Nijinsky will ever be paid. As I have said, whenever people talk about the great horses of all time they will talk of Nijinsky . . . and Lester Piggott. We were lucky enough to witness this super duo.

CHAPTER FOURTEEN

'I fear him like the plague'

The year 1970 will always be remembered as the year of
Nijinsky and Piggott – an all-conquering double act the like
of which we may never see again. But it would be very
wrong to think that this was the only success for the champion during the year. He achieved many things besides the
Triple Crown on Nijinsky, and one was extremely rare . . .
he silenced controversial bookmaker John Banks for 20
minutes which must be a record in itself. Usually the flame-
haired Scotsman says more in 20 minutes than tight-lipped
Lester utters in a year. But when the Lincoln was run at the
start of the 1970 Flat season campaign Lester left 'Banksie'
speechless.

At just about the same time that a young wonder boy
called Lester was exploding on to the racing scene in the late
forties another youngster was growing up in the slums of
Glasgow. His name was John Banks. It's history now how
the youngster used to put on bets with illegal street bookmakers for his father on his way to watch his beloved
Rangers every Saturday. From those modest beginnings one
of the best bookmaker's rags-to-riches stories of all time was
born. John eventually worked for a bookmaker and much
of his first racing experience was gained after his father
had lifted him over the turnstiles at Hamilton Park. 'Bookmakers just fascinated me,' John told me once. 'When I
went racing in those early days I just could not stop myself
looking at them.' From Glasgow John moved to Newcastle
and it was while he was there that he paid £14,000 for the
Schweppes Hurdle winner Hill House, who was trained by

149

Ryan Price at Findon. Most people told Banks that he was a prize mug to pay this figure for the horse who made his own dope. 'But it was the greatest thing I ever did,' John said. 'I was soon known as John Banks the man who paid all that dough for Hill House. I got to be known.'

From Newcastle John came further south, and at the start of the 1970 season he had arrived. Hated by some of his bookmaking colleagues for his statement that betting shops were money factories, Banks became the bookie everybody was talking about. And that's just what he wanted. When he opened his Lincoln ante-post lists he quoted Prince de Galles at 100–8. As the weeks went by he had plenty of bets on the Prince and on the day of the race he worked out that if Prince de Galles won it would cost him £128,000. What must surely have worried him even more was the fact that Prince de Galles, now backed down to a warm favourite, was being partnered by Lester Piggott. Banks has always claimed that Ladbroke's and their shrewd chief Cyril Stein were behind much of the ante-post money. They clearly did not like the way Banks was becoming the blue-eyed boy of the southern tracks.

When the day of the race arrived Banks was his usual flamboyant self before the race, even though he knew he had such a pile of money to pay out if Lester won. Having started at 16–1 originally, the Prince went to post 9–4 favourite. He made a great challenge but failed to give Lester his first Lincoln after 13 tries. After New Chapter, trained by Lester's father-in-law Sam Armstrong and ridden by Scotsman Sandy Barclay, had flashed past the post at 100–9, Banks must have thought that 13 was a very lucky number. Then came the horrifying shock – Lester, who had finished second, had objected to the winner. He claimed that New Chapter had 'bumped and bored him throughout the final furlong'. It was another Piggott-Barclay clash in the stewards' room.

For 20 minutes Banks was silent. He strolled off to a quiet corner of the racecourse with his closest friend in racing, his trainer Frank Carr. 'I wanted to get somewhere out of the way where the public couldn't see my knees knocking,' said Banks afterwards. Later the announcement came that the objection had been overruled. Piggott had still not won the Lincoln and Banks had won about £28,000 instead of having to pay out a staggering £128,000. 'It would not have wrecked me,' Banks said, 'but it would have taken the smile off my face for a decade.' Instead it was Ladbroke's who had the long faces.

Banks won over £20,000 in bets when Lester won the Royal Hunt Cup on his Kamundu at 7–1 in 1969. He has every reason to appreciate the talents of Lester. But as I strolled round Banks' palatial Sunningdale home one Sunday I asked him about the other side of the Banks-Piggott combination. That of Banks the bookie and Piggott the rider. Banks was quick to tell me: 'He's a menace. He's done me very well when he has ridden for me, but I have to say that he is a menace. No bookmaker can afford to rule him out. As a bookmaker I want to be where he is. There's no doubt that wherever Lester is riding the crowd is up and that means that the bookmakers take more money. As an owner I love him. As a bookmaker I fear him like the plague. I think that racecourses should pay him appearance money. I have sponsored a few races and the first thing the track concerned asks me always is whether Piggott will be there on the day. He can cost the bookmakers a cool £1 million every time he rides a treble. I have seen him some days ride a double or treble and I am convinced that sometimes he rides like a man possessed. I know him quite well but you would not call us friends. Even when he won on Kamundu he only muttered a couple of words after the race and then dashed off.

John Banks also told me that he thinks that Lester is 10 lbs superior to any other jockey. 'All the jockeys know that he is the guv'nor. If I am at a meeting and suddenly it's announced that Piggott is riding a horse which was 4–1, I immediately quote it at 5–2. This really puts fear in any bookmaker. As I say, I want to capitalize where Piggott is riding. If he is riding a professional might have £100 on a horse. If it was any other jockey he would probably only have £50. This guy creates an atmosphere and that's why he should be paid extra for appearing. When he has three or four winners it costs the bookmakers a fortune. I have had losing days when Lester has cost me over £12,000. So what does he do to the big boys like Hill's? I am a man of many words, Lester is not. Sometimes I do not think we are compatible. But at the same time I have nothing but admiration for him. He may be a menace every day I go on to a racecourse but it's his professionalism that I love. There's no racing life without Lester.'

Roy Sutterlin, who controls the credit betting side of the giant William Hill Organization, outlined to me the effect Piggott can have on the betting industry. He told me: 'When Lester has a winner it is bound to have been backed quite heavily. If he starts to multiply his winners that's when the fun starts. If he has a double or treble we have so much money going on the next legs that the starting prices are bound to be smaller as we ring money back to the course. If he has a treble or even a four-timer the amount of money going on his horses is gigantic. There's no doubt that he can cause us a few headaches but at the same time it is true that he is so popular that probably there will not be many long-priced Piggott winners in the course of the season.'

Despite riding some of the top fillies of his time Lester never won the 1,000 Guineas until 1970 and that was on a chance ride. Peter Walwyn would normally have given stable jockey Duncan Keith the ride on Humble Duty. But Keith had been unlucky where Lester had survived. Duncan had big weight problems and his near starvation diet resulted in an illness before the 1970 season. So Piggott, a man with a weight problem to beat them all, snapped up a winning 1,000 ride because of another. Stories of Lester's meanness are legend. But Duncan Keith can quote a good example to the contrary. 'After I had watched Humble Duty win on television, I received a case of champagne from Lester,' he recalls.

In May Lester scored a fluent win on the super mare Park

Top in the £6,600 Prix la Coupe at Longchamp. The Duke of Devonshire's mare swept past her three French challengers in grand style to win by half a length. Later that year the same combination scored another big success at Ascot to rival the thrilling victory the previous year in the King George VI and Queen Elizabeth Stakes from outsiders Crozier and Hogarth. But if it was cheers at Ascot it was the sad sound of booing at Longchamp in October when Piggott was thought to have ridden an ill-judged race in the Prix Royallieu. Lester was booed, jeered and slow-hand-clapped by the angry crowd after Park Top had dead-heated for third place behind Prime Abord. If it had not been such a tragic occasion one could have been forgiven for a slight smile when the Duke of Devonshire gave the French crowd a clear-cut message of his feelings towards their behaviour. In the best of Churchillian and Harvey Smith style he stuck two fingers in the air, causing an even greater squeal from the crowd. Trainer Bernard van Cutsem and Piggott were both interviewed by the stewards. They said that the soft ground did not seem to suit Park Top.

Lester did have one encouraging race that afternoon when he rode David Robinson's My Swallow to victory for the eighth consecutive time. He had scored on the impressive colt on Derby Day and this was yet another conclusive victory. At 100–30 on My Swallow proved that his narrow victory over Mill Reef – also in France – was no fluke. After Lester and My Swallow had led almost throughout the one-mile test to win by a comfortable half-length from Bonami I remember wondering to myself as I flew back to London whether this would be the Derby 'hot pot' for 1971. When David Robinson announced in the autumn that Frankie Durr would be retained as his first jockey for the following season it was also stated that Piggott would always ride My Swallow. But when I visited Frankie at his home he told me: 'Racing is a funny game. I expect that I will ride My Swallow on the racecourses. I schooled him throughout the starting stalls and I think that he's quite an outstanding colt.' My Swallow won £80,000 as a two-year-old which was a record.

As the winter months arrived it was obvious that Lester would be champion again, and he was with 162 winners. But he also rode winners in other countries. His 'away' score was France 44, Ireland 2. For the first time in his long career the rumours of bad health were common and it came as no surprise at the end of the season when he said, 'Doctors have advised me to have a rest.' After his ride in the Laurel race he flew to Puerto Rico and the bookmakers announced that Geoff Lewis, who was to take over from Sandy Barclay as Noel Murless's stable jockey, was 5–4-on favourite for the jockeys' title. Lester was evens. After many years of continual wasting and dieting the pace had finally begun to tell. He was forced to give Lewis his invitation rides in Australia for December and January.

I never cease to be amazed by one of Lester's driving finishes when he has ridden a waiting race. It thrills me also to see him judge the speed of a race and then slip the field like he did so successfully in the Cesarewitch on Major Rose in 1968. Sheer perfection! The way he goes through the Classic field and then selects one horse which eventually turns out to be the winner is further proof of his masterful mind. There are many things about this man which amaze you and prove a point of discussion until the early hours. But for me the most amazing thing about Lester is the fact that for over a dozen years he has constantly been forced to watch his weight. Through all the glory years he has lived like a starving prisoner on the run. His wealth is such that he could throw a banquet every night of the year at the Savoy. Instead there is so much determination and drive inside this remarkable man that he goes on and on. His self-discipline has to be seen to be believed. 'Of course it's not true that I just smoke big cigars to kill my hunger pains,' says Lester, who also likes to point out that he does not dive into the *Financial Times* every time he climbs out of bed in the morning. But stories of Lester's wasting are not untrue. Other jockeys have to cut down on their food. Other jockeys have to spend horrible hours in sauna baths. But no jockey in the land, or in the history of this great sport, has ever gone through the near torture that this man endures. On Lester's dining-room table at Newmarket is a figurehead of that outstanding jockey Fred Archer. As Lester eats his almost non-existent meals he can gaze up at that face. It must be in his mind that Fred Archer had such a terrible problem with his weight that it finally drove him to shoot himself.

Jimmy Lindley probably had as big a weight problem as anybody in the game. But he admitted to me: 'I had to lose several pounds at times. But I could never waste like Lester. I could get down to 8 st 7 lb, which should be about as low as Lester can go. But, oh no, he can get down to 8 st 4 lb and even lower. It is really quite amazing. Like me, I suppose that if we worked in an office and had nothing to do with racing our weights would be well over 10 stone. I had a strict diet and went in for a lot of sauna baths. I built one on to my house. Lester is different. He is purely a diet boy. Sometimes when it got pretty close I can tell you that Lester and myself could really feel the wind whistling through us. It really tucks you up a little.' Another jockey told me: 'Would you walk around grinning like a Cheshire cat if you were starving yourself all summer?' It's this constant self-control in the battle of the bulge which accounts for a great deal in Lester's make-up. Peter O'Sullevan and I were discussing some of the big names in racing one day when he remarked: 'Lester amazes me. How he can keep up this constant wasting is a mystery. I'm sure that's why he is not always as talkative as he might be.'

But until Lester quits he will never let up on this way of life which would wreck lesser men. He will still make long journeys in a suit and heavy overcoat with the windows of his car tightly closed and the radiator full on. Some jockeys have a break now and again from the daily diet. Jimmy Lindley tells me that jockeys always regard Monday as 'Black Monday' as it usually means that they have had a day off the previous day and might have had a little to eat. Whatever they have put on over the weekend must be sweated off!

Lester's sacrifice will go on until the very end. He could never accept a situation where he was anything else but the tops. I can understand when Geoff Lewis says: 'I would love to be champion when the big fella is around. To be champion when Lester had retired would not mean a thing.'

When Lester sunned himself on the beaches of Puerto Rico during the winter months of 1970–1 there were many people who contacted their bookmakers and accepted the odds-on price that was being asked about Geoff Lewis for the jockeys' title.

This is the classic reason why the bookmakers get richer and the punter gets poorer. The public should have known. Tall, pale Lester's will-to-win made a mockery of doctor's advice. His diet would fill graveyards right, left and centre. Instead it drives him to limits of self-discipline no other sportsman has ever mastered.

CHAPTER FIFTEEN

Racing's luckless Prince

Fleet Street racing writers always like to be armed with good feature stories when the bad weather wrecks the winter programme. So my enthusiasm for being at Newmarket early in 1971 is easily explained.

Back in Fleet Street I had thought it would be a good idea to get a picture and short story on a particular two-year-old on January 1st – all horses' birthday.

My choice was soon made easy when I heard that Bernard van Cutsem, the late trainer, had taken possession of the world's then record-priced yearling, Crowned Prince, who cost 510,000 dollars. He was a brother to Kentucky Derby winner Majestic Prince and had been purchased amid great publicity at Keeneland Yearling Sales and then flown to Bernard van Cutsem's Stanley House stables just off the Bury Road at Newmarket. One quick 'phone call to this helpful trainer and I had my appointment, a meeting which interested me not only as a good story and picture, but also as the chance to be one of the first Englishmen to see the animal.

At 10 o'clock, as arranged, the photographer and myself ventured into the fabulous Stanley House stables, made famous in racing history by the horses of Lord Derby. As the clock above the archway in the middle of the yard struck ten, Bernard van Cutsem arrived from his nearby Exning home. A carpet of snow covered the yard. The stage was set for a sight I will never forget.

We made our way to horsebox No. 3 as van Cutsem told me: 'This box was previously occupied by Karabas and

Park Top.' When he unbolted the heavy padlock and opened the door we saw the magnificent big chestnut. I found it hard to visualize any man paying a quarter of a million pounds in hard cash for a horse. But when I saw this good-looking fellow I could see the way a millionaire's mind could work. This was a really outstanding-looking horse.

As it had been snowing quite a lot just previously van Cutsem had ordered one of his stable lads to line the path to Crowned Prince's indoor exercise area with straw. Eventually Crowned Prince stepped out in the crisp January daylight. What power, I remember commenting.

But van Cutsem was quick to spot my enthusiasm, and warned: 'You must not think that just because he cost so much he is going to be a great racehorse. Many big buys have been complete flops. It's a gamble in many ways.

'But I must confess he does look a little extra ... and his first visitor here thought so, too. We had a visit from Lester Piggott the other night. He didn't waste any time in getting round to see him.

'He thought that Crowned Prince looked an outstanding two-year-old.'

The news of Piggott's early visit did not surprise me, but the size and well-being of the horse did. As he looked around intelligently and took little notice of the camera clicking he looked more like a three-year-old. The lad who 'did' the horse goes by the name of John Banks, though he's no relation. He was obviously as pleased as anything with his new companion. 'He's as good as gold,' he said, and left an obvious quote for my story.

Would it be an extra responsibility training a horse worth all this money? Where would he have his first race? Had Piggott actually asked to ride the horse? These were the obvious questions I asked van Cutsem and he answered them in his usual open manner.

Van Cutsem was true to his word, and it was Newmarket where Crowned Prince finally graced the racecourse. His trainer had selected a 19-runner maiden in August and the appearance of this record buy must have nearly doubled the attendance.

Although he had never been on a racetrack, Crowned Prince was already a top draw in the Mill Reef, Nijinsky and Arkle class. Bookmakers were obviously not going to join in the celebration of seeing the new talking-point of racing in action as they chalked up 7–2 on. I saw more than one big punter plunging in, no doubt thinking that any horse costing that much money must be a good thing. Added to this was the opinion expressed by van Cutsem some days before that the horse had been producing some absolutely brilliant performances at home.

John Oaksey, always a man to find the best words for such an occasion, was commentating on ITV for the race. As he saw Lester Piggott and Crowned Prince standing relaxed at the start, he likened the favourite to 'a hunter'. It was a good description.

As I made my way up to the Press area high in the Newmarket stands I reflected to myself that this surely had to be the biggest certainty of all time. Why what actually happened in the race did will be a mystery van Cutsem, Piggott and thousands of racegoers and TV viewers will never know. Two furlongs from home Piggott moved up to the leaders as though he would win as he liked. When the pace quickened and he asked Crowned Prince for a little more he was forced to give the colt a little reminder. From that moment he seemed to be going backwards as the other horses raced to the line. It was one of the most remarkable races I've ever seen. Afterwards the faces of Piggott and van Cutsem told the story. Their high-priced hope had been beaten out of sight by moderate buys.

Later, Piggott told me: 'He ran green. He'll be the better for the race.' I got the impression from the champion as I spoke to him over the 'phone that he was not as worried as I thought he would have been. And when I made contact with van Cutsem, as Crowned Prince had enjoyed a good spin at Yarmouth racecourse, I got the distinct feeling that the horse must have made considerable improvement.

When van Cutsem announced that Crowned Prince would run in blinkers in his next race, probably the Champagne Stakes at Doncaster, his critics really went to town. The expression 'rogue's mask' was very free as people tried to work out why a Classic contender, worth more money than most men could earn in 100 years, was going to have to resort to blinkers. Trainers I spoke to agreed that Crowned Prince might improve if he wore blinkers, and in the Champagne Stakes we did indeed see a different Crowned Prince. Looking superb he lived up to his big reputation and price and slaughtered his rivals. Lester sent him to the front and he had the others completely shattered a long way from home. Crowned Prince's critics changed their tune – well, at least, most of them did. That day he was eased up a little towards the end of the race and still had a length to spare over strong-finishing Rheingold. He started a warm odds-on favourite.

And he was to be odds-on for the third successive time when he made his last appearance of 1971 in the Dewhurst Stakes at Newmarket. Yet again he pulled the crowd to Newmarket. As I drove up from London, I had the feeling that nearly every car was heading towards the course to see this remarkable two-year-old and that equally remarkable 35-year-old Lester Piggott. People realized that Piggott's Classic programme seemed to revolve around Crowned Prince and they were not going to miss any development which would make the champion change his mind. The year of 1971 had been the year of Mill Reef, Brigadier Gerard, Geoff Lewis and Joe Mercer. Now the champion was going to get a clear-cut form line to the Classics of 1972, and thousands didn't want to miss it.

In 1970 the Dewhurst Stakes, worth £10,000 to the winner, had gone to Mill Reef, who had been a 7–4 on favourite in the hands of Geoff Lewis. Now Crowned Prince was backed down to odds-on. And as I watched him enter the parade ring followed by van Cutsem and his wife Mini, looking extremely pensive, I couldn't help feeling that this chap was bigger and better than the rest. Gone were the blinkers, gone were most of the suspicions that he was the record-price let-down of all time. I suspect that many race-goers, like myself, wanted to see a really outstanding display that day to warm our hearts throughout the winter. We were not to be disappointed.

Unlike the Doncaster event, Lester kept Crowned Prince in the centre of the field and did not force his way to the front. Gone now were the strained looks on van Cutsem and his wife. Crowned Prince had proved beyond all doubt that he was class, not a duffer. He could not have been more impressive and, of course, bookmaking representatives were quickly on the scene to quote ante-post prices for the following year's Guineas and Derby. They made it 5–2 for the first and 4–1 for the second.

As I said, nearly everyone who knew anything about racing forgave and forgot that first display at Newmarket. After his third victory van Cutsem told me: 'I'm extremely pleased he had done everything today that we wanted him to do. I ran him at Doncaster in blinkers because we wanted to teach him to race. In his first race he was green and looking around like a big baby. The blinkers taught him that you just can't charge after the others. He's learned his lesson.'

With that, van Cutsem and his delighted party went away for a celebration drink. In their minds there remained no doubts whatsoever. Here was a Classic horse passing one of his last exams with flying colours before getting ready for the two bigger tests.

The one aspect of the Dewhurst which gave me concern was that David Robinson's Wishing Star had won the Gim-crack Stakes from Philip of Spain, but had been well down the field against Crowned Prince. Did that make the Dew-hurst good form or bad? Bill Marshall's Mercia Boy, who had previously run six times without getting into the winner's enclosure, was able to fight his way into the picture not many lengths behind Crowned Prince. These are the questions only the winter months and an initial spin on the racecourse can answer. But for my money Crowned Prince was highly impressive in the Dewhurst, in the same way Mill

Reef was the previous year. Lester Piggott would, of course, receive invitations to ride any one of a dozen horses in the 1972 Classics. I think, though, that it would have had to be something a little special to make him turn his attention from the colt he visited at van Cutsem's yard just after Christmas in 1970, only a few hours after the American-bred newcomer had landed in this country.

When the Flat season closed on October 31st, 1971, I revisited van Cutsem to assess his hopes for the coming year. Rather like the Cox and Box comic opera, Lester Piggott's path and mine had just crossed. Piggott was due to fly off to South Africa for invitation races the Sunday after the Manchester Handicap. But in the morning he had made a last visit to see Crowned Prince and van Cutsem. From Newmarket I 'phoned this story to the *Sun*:

'The lone figure who walked into the Stanley House Stables at Newmarket just after Christmas last year to see the new occupant of box No. 3 was back again yesterday.

'For Lester Piggott and Bernard van Cutsem it was the crucial chat of the year.

'And, once again, the reason for Lester's visit was the magnificent chestnut occupying the box formerly used by Karabas and Park Top . . . Crowned Prince.

'After winning the jockeys' title for the eighth successive year Piggott was talking things over with van Cutsem before flying off to South Africa for invitation races. It's odds-on that they discussed the 1972 Classics and the vice-like grip van Cutsem seems to have on the big cash prizes Piggott yearns to win.

'The trainer told me of his hopes for his super string of two-year-olds who made a near monopoly of their leading races in 1971. He said: "At the start of the season I knew we had some pretty nice two-year-olds. But I never guessed that we would be so fortunate and have 35 two-year-old winners. You dream of such success but rarely achieve it.

' "Seeing Crowned Prince (Dewhurst Stakes), High Top (Observer Gold Cup) and Sharpen Up (Middle Park Stakes) **all win was a tremendous thrill, but to see Lester Piggott win** on Crowned Prince was the highlight. That's because it was always an extra responsibility training this one with the financial aspect always in the back of your mind.

' "Training a horse worth all that money was a tremendous responsibility. But make no mistake. I know some people still have doubts. But this is a bloody good horse. People who have been saying that this and that are still wrong will be getting a pretty sharp message from me.

' "All three are entered in the 2,000 Guineas. Crowned Prince is also entered for the French and Irish 2,000 and Sharpen Up only for the English 2,000. I could have quite a problem choosing which horse for which race. But these things usually sort themselves out. It will be interesting to see how the horses winter. I want a mild open winter. You never know one of the horses could come on quicker than the others.

' "If Crowned Prince does go for the 2,000 I imagine that he would have one race beforehand. I suppose it's true to say that Lester Piggott probably does see Crowned Prince as his best hope for the 1972 Derby. We have an understanding that he will ride him. Lester is very keen to do so.

' "I also have an above average filly in Carezza. She was magnificent in winning her first race at Newbury in September, beating 26 others. She is bred to get one and a half miles and I think she will prove that she has that little bit extra." '

We are stuck with these kind of prices whenever Piggott teams up with a would-be Guineas or Derby winner. It's the price we pay for trying to cash in on the genius of the man.

Sadly, the Crowned Prince story, which I expected to be climaxed at Epsom with thousands of racegoers cheering in his ears, came to a sensational end on deserted Yarmouth racecourse. Crowned Prince, hot favourite for the 2,000 Guineas and Derby, ran a shocking race in the 1972 Craven at Newmarket, when he finished an almost unbelievable fourth. Van Cutsem told me sadly, 'He didn't race very well, did he?' He was clearly greatly shocked.

The suggestion that Crowned Prince had a soft palate was

confirmed when Lester Piggott partnered the massive colt on a trial spin at Yarmouth. Plans were immediately made for Crowned Prince to go to stud in Ireland, and one of the most dramatic chapters of would-be classic victory was closed.

For Piggott, who thought he was an outstanding colt, he will always be remembered as the Uncrowned Prince.

CHAPTER SIXTEEN

'No word from Mount Sinai'

At the end of the 1970 season Lester Piggott was champion for the sixth time in succession with 162 winners. He was tired, weary and ready for a few weeks' holiday in the Caribbean and the Bahamas. At the end of the 1971 season Lester was champion again, making a mockery of those who said that his legend had ground to a halt amid continual wasting. He had ridden 162, the same as the previous year. Nothing had changed – he was as great as ever.

But Lester was never champion again after 1971. The King of the Turf abdicated his title. The day to day slog was over and he concentrated on the big races. Willie Carson (1972, 1973) and then Pat Eddery became champions. Lester was no longer King but he still ruled over his fellow jockeys.

Before the start of the 1971 season I visited Geoff Lewis at his home in Burgh Heath. Thrilled about the prospect of riding for Noel Murless, he said: 'This is the year I beat Lester for the title. I have been runner-up for two successive seasons. Now I really think that I can do it, although I know that it's the hardest job in racing. He's so dedicated and will travel day and night to ride in a seller. You can't afford to miss one evening meeting, he'll be there. We are, of course, good friends, but we have never once talked about the jockeys' championship. Even when we were having that terrible battle in 1970, he never discussed the title, not even in fun. Lester doesn't talk about these sort of things.'

Geoff told me the story of his row with Lester in 1969 as they rode for all they were worth up the straight at Sandown.

He said: 'That's one thing about Lester, he's so cool. You can never draw him out. After I had that little go with him and the whips were exchanged we were both fined £50. As he hit me first I joked that he should pay my fine. He just laughed and walked away.'

Although Geoff was badly injured on the day of the 2,000 Guineas at Newmarket near the start of the 1971 season, you could say that he had the last laugh that season. Probably for the first time since Gordon Richards retired in 1953 there was another jockey who was talked about and mentioned in headlines as often as Lester. For Geoff had a remarkable year on Mill Reef, winning every race he raced in apart from the 2,000 Guineas. Joe Mercer enjoyed similar success on Brigadier Gerard and their clash in the 1972 Eclipse was billed as the race of the century but, sadly, it never took place. These super colts only once stepped into the same ring together and then it was the Brigadier who scored a clear-cut points victory.

As I have said, Lester was champion again in 1971. Throughout the season it was Willie Carson and Tony Murray who followed the champion's trail. At the start of the season it seemed likely that Lewis and Frankie Durr would press him most. But in one afternoon at Newmarket Lewis was badly injured and Durr was suspended for a month for rough riding. Halfway through the season Lester told a rival of mine that he thought Carson was a certainty for the title. It must have been one of the biggest leg-pulls of all time.

Lester's season started with the shock news that he would not be riding My Swallow in the Guineas. I was visiting Ian Balding at his Kingsclere stables when it was announced. 'With all due respect to Frankie Durr you can say that I am delighted to hear the news,' said Ian, whose training of Mill Reef throughout a long and difficult season must rate as one of the finest training jobs of them all.

Lester rode Nijinsky's brother Minsky in the Guineas but had no success. His Derby mount at one time was the Ryan Price colt Levanter, who had turned in a top-class display at

Newmarket. Levanter was not so clever at the tricky Chester circuit and was later declared a Classic non-runner. Irish Ball was once thought to be Piggott's Epsom mount but he finally opted for The Parson, who was trained by Noel Murless. I think that this was Lester's selection from the pick of a poor bunch. 'If Mill Reef stays he is a certainty,' Lester said before the race, and yet again his big-race prediction came true. The Parson would have been the first maiden to have won the Derby for dozens of years but Lester was never in a position to win. In a rare outburst at the Curragh in May, Lester threatened to boycott Irish racing after the 2,000 Guineas. His mount Sparkler was beaten a neck by Freddie Head and King's Company. Lester objected on the grounds that he was hampered. 'I will never race here again if I do not get this race,' said an angry Lester. 'I was murdered for more than a furlong and a half.' After the stewards had announced that the placings would remain unaltered French champion Head said: 'Lester is no fool. When he saw that I had him beaten he put on an act. I never touched him.'

But Lester went back again to Ireland. Racing men seem to have short memories, or is it the thought of missing out on a big prize that makes them overlook a previous statement? Among the well-known trainers both Paddy Prendergast and Noel Murless have sworn that Lester would never ride for them again. He did so for both.

If Lester was easing up nobody noticed it in 1971. He ended the season with a farewell flurry at Haydock, riding a tremendous treble that showed every superb skill and power that this man can call upon. His victory on Green God was particularly fine. In his previous race the David Robinson speedster had strayed off a straight line and had been disqualified although finishing first. Here Lester showed his genius by keeping Green God perfectly straight as a big end-of-season gamble was successfully won.

Yet again he had ridden 162 winners. Yet again he had shown that as a freelance he could still show all his rivals the way home.

That night I dined with some well-known jockeys as we broke the journey back south. The name of Lester was bound to crop up and of course it did. 'Do you know?' said one of Lester's main rivals, 'they say he's mean. That's not true. He's twice as mean as they say. They say he's difficult to get on with. That's not true either. He's impossible to make real friends with. And they say he's great. That's certainly not true. He's the greatest jockey the world will ever see. Great will never describe him, he's too good for that.'

As far as records are concerned it is true that the immortal Fred Archer does have outstanding claims to be called the best of them all. He rode 21 Classic winners and during his 13-year reign as champion he eight times topped the 200 mark. In 1885 he rode 246 winners. Many will say that Gordon Richards, who was champion 26 times and rode 4,870 winners, was the best jockey. Some of the old-timers insist there were others who would rank among the all-time greats. We should not forget Steve Donoghue, who was champion from 1914 to 1922 and shared the title in 1923. He is another who will be talked about when people are discussing the outstanding jockeys.

I never saw the likes of Donoghue and Archer. I have seen Richards and Piggott and I refuse to believe that there can ever have been a man on a horse to match Lester. Moody, often misunderstood, gifted ... this is Piggott. Give him an ordinary personality like anybody in the street and the great Piggott mystery ends. He remains a household name who nobody really knows. Talk to all the people close to him and still there are precious few examples of the real Piggott. All the people who know Piggott have one thing in common – they all rate him the greatest.

Frank Durr is one of them. He told me: 'Of course he's the greatest of all time. But when you walk out of the changing room alongside him you have to forget all of that. Let's face it, if you go out to the track and believe that Lester is so much better than you there's no point going out. People say that he hasn't a sense of humour but he has — a special sort of his own. I remember one day I was driving down

Newmarket High Street on my way to Wolverhampton races with Derek Morris. I saw that we were following Lester's chauffeur and we flagged him down.

'He explained that he had to pick Lester up at a certain point but when he arrived Lester was not to be seen. As the time was getting on I suggested that he must have gone by other means and we climbed into the car and I left mine. Derek and I got changed for the races but there was no sign of Lester. Then suddenly he came running in, fuming with rage. He had arrived at the meeting point just in time to see his chauffeur-driven car roaring off with me and Derek sitting comfortably in the back. He had been forced to hire a car and sacked the chauffeur on the spot. He was livid. But he rode a double and then made it a treble. After that he joked about it and forgave the chauffeur.'

Is he really as keen on money as they say? I'm afraid so. Sally Masson, wife of the Lewes trainer, told me of the time they were in France for Lester to ride Sir Charles Clore's Varma. The horse duly obliged and the trainer and his wife were taking a taxi to the airport. 'When we were stopped at a crossroad Lester, who was in a taxi nearby, spotted us. He just jumped out of his taxi and in with us,' she said. 'I thought it was extremely funny, but the other taxi driver wasn't so happy.'

Does he never break out and have a decent meal? Says Jimmy Lindley: 'At the York meeting every year, Lester, Joe Mercer and myself have a special little dinner party. You should see Lester tucking in to the grouse, he loves it. But he never has any vegetables. There is always some horse he is riding the next day, which he keeps thinking about.'

His father, Keith Piggott, says: 'If he has a cup of tea, he only drinks half of it. If he goes to a celebration dinner after some winner he has ridden, he'll have a glass of champagne. But he'll only ever drink half of it. I've never seen him finish a glass of anything in the last 15 years. It's just his way of life.'

After Lester had stormed home on Crowned Prince in the Dewhurst Stakes at Newmarket in 1971, I gathered with other racing journalists round the spot allotted for the winner. Piggott dismounted and ran off to get weighed in. He reacted as though he had just won another race and not as though his 1972 Classic plans might have been finalized by this victory.

'Has there been any word from God yet?' one seasoned journalist asked of Crowned Prince's trainer, Bernard van Cutsem. 'No, there has been no word from Mount Sinai,' said van Cutsem solemnly. Among the top Newmarket trainers, the men who have prepared so many of his winners, Lester's nickname is 'God'. That's how highly he is rated. I know of no other sportsman who has this honour. Piggott is unique.

The most clear-cut example of Piggott's supremacy over his rivals came on the eve of the 1972 Derby. Lester's name had been linked with several colts after Crowned Prince's shock exit. Yet although Bill Williamson said he was fully fit to ride Roberto after falling badly a few days previously, it was Lester who obtained the winning ride. I say 'obtained' because public opinion was firm that Lester went out of his way to get the ride. Williamson had to watch from the stands as Lester won his sixth Derby. I reported the race as the 'Silent Derby', because of the hushed reception in the winner's enclosure.

People will always say that Williamson was terribly wronged. Years later in Melbourne I chatted to Bill's wife Zelma about the 'jockeying off'. She said, 'Susan Piggott came up afterwards and said "sorry". That was nice. What hurt Bill and I so much was that all jockeys dream of winning the Derby and at the age of 50 this was obviously Bill's best and last chance'.

To give Bill Williamson the £6,000 prize-money percentage meant little to the Aussie. But one fact cannot be argued: with a devastating finish spotlighting his immense power, Piggott won a neck-and-neck duel with Ernie Johnson on Rheingold. Eleven times in the desperate final furlong Lester's whip flashed on Roberto. He certainly stole the glory from Rheingold and justified the owner and trainer's last minute switch of jockeys. Nobody but the great Lester Piggott could have done it. No other jockey in living memory would have won that race on Roberto.

I remember chatting with Ryan Price just after Roberto's win. 'Lester would have won on the runner-up,' I said. 'Don't be a bloody fool, my boy,' roared Ryan. 'He'd have won on the ruddy fifth!'

CHAPTER SEVENTEEN

Rheingold ends the Arc agony

Master trainers Sir Noel Murless and Vincent O'Brien supplied Lester Piggott with the ammunition to fire his Classic salvos. Year after year he blasted his rivals and such was his grip on the Classics that he could have been reported to the Monopolies Commission. But the Prix de l'Arc de Triomphe, until October 7, 1973, remained the one glittering prize yet to be won by the 'Long Fella.'

So often Lester's dreams of winning the world's richest race had been dashed. Critics slammed him for his riding of Park Top and Nijinsky. In the scramble in the straight in the Arc the winner always has to be in the leading group. But on both those horses Piggott tried to come from behind and both times he was pipped.

Now Rheingold, rated by Lester only behind Sir Ivor and Nijinsky as his favourites, proved to be the pot of gold at the end of the Paris rainbow. And it proved to be a fairy-tale for owner Henry Zeisel, one-time leading violinist in the Vienna Philharmonic Orchestra. For years his fingers had produced magical moments of music. Those same cultured hands were now to lead in Lester's first Arc winner.

Zeisel's first opera as lead violinist of the Vienna Orchestra – at the age of only 17 – was the Wagner-composed Rheingold. The conductor was the legendary Italian Toscanini. Henry booted home 11 point-to-point winners in the sixties. He named his charming London night-club after Rheingold, and similarly the 3,000-guinea yearling Barry Hills bought on his behalf ... his first ever Flat horse. Recalls Henry: 'He wasn't very spectacular as a yearling. He was a bit gangling but had lovely clear eyes and that's what made me say, "He's for me".'

First time out at Newcastle in 1971 Rheingold landed a huge gamble. Then he was second to Crowned Prince in the Champagne Stakes. Piggott was on the subsequently disappointing Crowned Prince then but it was the runner-up who was to become one of his favourites. Crowned Prince also beat Rheingold into second place in the Dewhurst. Then he was seventh in the Observer Gold Cup behind High Top.

As a three-year-old Rheingold, always ridden by Ernie Johnson in those days, won at Redcar in heavy going and then was beaten by Scottish Rifle in a blanket finish in the Blue Riband at Epsom. But even after he had won the Date, Hills was not sure that he was up to Derby standards. Says Zeisel: 'He thought that he was just a top-class handicapper. But I met Phil Bull and he said that Rheingold only had one chance to win the Derby and I should take it.'

On the eve of the 1972 Derby, Zeisel sold 80% of Rheingold to a syndicate which included Tim Sasse, Charles St George and Peter Richards. It's history now that Rheingold was pipped in the Derby by Piggott on Roberto. Says Zeisel: 'With the greatest respect to Ernie Johnson I must say that if Lester had been on Rheingold he would have won the Derby. Rheingold hung and Ernie did not change his whip-hand.'

Twice Rheingold won the Grand Prix de Saint-Cloud; in fact he was never beaten on French soil. But it was the 1973 Benson and Hedges Gold Cup when he ran as a four-year-old that put Rheingold back in the headlines ... for the wrong reasons.

Piggott was due to ride Roberto but he was pulled out at 7.30 a.m. because of the soft going. Vincent O'Brien was fined £100. At 10 a.m. the Piggott brain was ticking over at full speed – he contacted Harry Wragg and obtained the ride on Moulton in place of Geoff Lewis. But at 1.25 he switched to Rheingold in place of Yves Saint-Martin and Lewis went back on Moulton.

Rheingold started at 6–4 on but flopped into third place

behind Moulton and a gleeful Lewis. This was the worst moment of Piggott's career and the crowd openly jeered when he returned to the winner's enclosure. The stewards announced: 'We deplore this action of changing jockeys.' Zeisel was bitterly opposed to the switch but was outvoted by the syndicate, who were very conspicuous by their absence near the colt after the race. Says Zeisel: 'I had just flown back from America and did not know about the jockeying off of Saint-Martin until I was on the train on the way to York.'

St George gives the other point of view. 'We had a contract with Piggott to ride Rheingold in the Arc,' he says. 'We also had an understanding that he would ride him whenever he was available. Saint-Martin was already booked to ride Allez France in the Arc so it was common sense to let Lester have his first ride on Rheingold.'

Lester, never over-worried about obtaining rides from his colleagues, said: 'Rheingold was a dead horse.' History showed that he was suffering from a blood disorder. He also had trouble with warts, and it was only the efforts of the late Syd Mercer that restored him.

The Rheingold affair left a terrible aftertaste. Saint-Martin was due 10% if Piggott won. But that did little to lessen the blow to the Frenchman's pride. But as Willie Carson says: 'Lester would nick anybody's ride. We all know it and have to accept it.'

In August the name of Rheingold was known for the 'jockeying off' affair. Racegoers had booed like mad. By October, in a typical racing turnabout, Rheingold was being greeted by delirious Englishmen in the winner's enclosure at Longchamp.

Says Zeisel: 'After York Barry Hills decided to give him an easy time. But a week before the Arc, Lester came down to Lambourn and worked on the colt. He went with Hickleton and Our Mirage in an uphill gallop. I watched early that morning and he absolutely flew. Lester said: "He's terrific".'

Hills, a one-time Newmarket head lad, contacted Ladbrokes and had a bet of £12,000 to £1,000 for the Arc. Lester recalls: 'Barry produced him trained to the minute for a race which was virtually a match between the great fillies Dahlia, who had beaten Rheingold in the King George VI, and Allez France.

'As soon as I got on Rheingold I knew he was ready to run the biggest race of his life. He was always a nice mover and I actually knew we could not be beaten as we went to the post.

'Rheingold did not want to come from too far back and I kept him handily placed all the way. Two furlongs out, as we hit the front, Rheingold jumped into a gear I have rarely seen, far less experienced. We literally charged to the line. We still had $2\frac{1}{2}$ lengths to spare over Allez France. I honestly do not think I ever sat on a horse that would have held Rheingold that day at Longchamp.'

The saddle Piggott used when he won the Arc is displayed in Henry Zeisel's club. Says Henry: 'At Newmarket sales after the Arc, Lester came over and bought me a bottle of champagne. That Arc win really did thrill him.

'I was very keen to lead Rheingold in. The ground was so holding that as I darted up to Lester and Rheingold I lost my shoe. Lester waited for me while I went back and put my shoe back on. He looked down and said, "A great horse. He's so brave." '

'The French press were so full of stories the next day that Lester actually smiled. After all his Arc disappointments I was thrilled that I owned the brave colt who gave him his first success in the race.

'Lester did not want to be advised before the race by us. But how could we tell this genius anything? He rode him his way. He is a master and still has great affection for Rheingold.

'That night we went off to a Russian restaurant and I borrowed a violin from the gypsy orchestra. I started playing and they told me the next day that I didn't stop for three hours. Lester made it all possible and I'll never forget that night if I live to be 100.'

I love the story of Zeisel and St George visiting Piggott at his Newmarket home after the Arc to deliver a cash token of their gratitude. Ironically, they had to wait outside while the jockey entertained the most famous name in the history of this great sport, Lord Derby. Piggott has virtually made the race his own but Lord Derby has not fulfilled his burning ambition to win the Epsom Classic, named after one of his forefathers.

Recalls Zeisel: 'We went in and gave Lester a nice present. Actually after Lester had been entertaining Lord Derby he had run out of champagne . . . so we had to drink cognac.'

Rheingold never raced again after the Arc. His bravery was highlighted by the fact that he injured tendons in the last desperate seconds of the race. His winning soared to well over £300,000, and he was then syndicated to Ireland for over £1 million thanks to St George's shrewd dealing.

As Zeisel says: 'Racing is a great leveller. I've met kings and beggars.'

Rheingold, bought because of his 'clear eyes', will always have special memories for Piggott. And he made a dream come true for the sporting violinist, who never forgot the Wagner fairytale.

CHAPTER EIGHTEEN

'I've never sat on a better horse'

Passing years will destroy the memory of many of Piggott's great triumphs. But the memory of Alleged's second win in the Arc de Triomphe will never fade. This was a combination of an outstanding horse, a master trainer, a big-spender and lucky owner ... and the genius of Piggott.

In Alleged's second Arc win at Longchamp on October 1, 1978, the whole racing world watched as Piggott's grip on the sport was demonstrated as never before. The moment the stalls flew open the entire race seemed to develop around him. 'He just mesmerized all the other jockeys,' said one onlooker, and he was dead right.

Maurice Zilber once told me: 'Piggott – he's the only jockey who knows pace. That's what racing is all about – pace.' A year previously Piggott had shown everybody what a brilliant tactician he is when making virtually every yard on Alleged out in front. This time he was never out of the first four. One felt that although this time he was not out ahead of his rivals he was still dictating the pace from behind.

After Alleged had streaked home two lengths ahead of Willie Shoemaker on Trillion, the memory of the after-race scenes in the tree-lined Longchamp paddock will never fade for those privileged to be present. Several of the beaten horses returned before a mighty roar, similar to the Romans' reception for a homecoming Caesar, which echoed around the vast stands.

Minutes later Lester emerged from the jockeys' room with a contented smile. He had earned £15,000 for less than three minutes' work, but the occasion of winning his third Arc meant just as much. Instantly surrounded by a possee of hacks, Piggott immediately made mention of Vincent O'Brien's remarkable training achievement. 'A fantastic performance,' said Lester. 'Six weeks ago there was a grave doubt whether Alleged would even run again this season.' When pressed about the greatness of Alleged Lester said: 'I've never sat on a better horse. He's super. You can do anything you like with him. I was a bit worried about the heavy rain which fell before the race but he won so easily. We had plenty in hand at the end.' Zilber launched an after-race tirade at Willie 'The Shoe' Shoemaker's riding of Trillion. While the filly did hang in the closing stages there was no way that Alleged was ever going to get beaten. Piggott manipulated the entire race like a master chess-player and it was obvious from the word go that his opponents would eventually end up in check-mate. 'Gee . . . that's some horse and some jockey,' the tiny 'Shoe' told me afterwards. 'My plan was to follow Piggott but when he kicked on in the straight I didn't have a prayer.'

This was Lester's third Arc de Triomphe win inside six years. The painful memories of his controversial rides on Park Top and Nijinsky – plus the expensive flop on Hard to Beat – were wiped out by Alleged's double success. As The Minstrel was syndicated for £6 million it was fair to assume that Alleged would probably become the first horse ever to near an eight-figure fee of £10 million. He was to become the superstud of all time.

In 1970, when the mighty Nijinsky was beaten for the first time in his life in the Arc, the antics of photographers were a disgrace. Lester will always claim that the milling pressmen who pestered Nijinsky before the race probably affected the wonder colt's display. When Alleged came back to the joyous reception in Paris there were similar problems. Cameramen standing five deep jostled like a rugby scrum, or Kop fans greeting a home goal. It must be recorded that the first words Piggott uttered after winning his unforgettable second Arc de Triomphe were a curt four-lettered rebuttal of the pressing photographers. Alleged stood almost motionless while scores of well-wishers rushed to greet Robert Sangster and Vincent O'Brien.

Only Ksar (1921–22), Corrida (1936–37), Tantiemme (1950–51) and Ribot (1956–57) had previously pulled off the remarkable Arc double. The legendary Ribot was indeed the great grandsire of Alleged. It was exactly 20 years before Alleged's triumph that O'Brien gained his first success in the Paris spectacular with Ballymoss.

With the Arc, Alleged had won nine out of his ten races. His only defeat was in the St Leger of 1977 when the ground was perhaps against him. Dunfermline, the Queen's filly, was also a top-class animal and there was no disgrace in the Doncaster defeat. Lester always maintained that he might have won the St Leger if he had not made all the running. Another of racing's great unanswered questions is whether Alleged actually stayed the full $1\frac{3}{4}$-mile St Leger distance. But after his second Arc de Triomphe win there was no doubt that Alleged was the champion of Europe at middle-distance races.

Before the 1978 Derby the originally much-fancied Try My Best finally came out of the picture, and the annual 'What does Lester ride?' puzzle game was under way. Sangster's Hawaiian Sound was a possibility, and his odds came tumbling down on pure speculation.

But Lester chose the O'Brien colt Inkerman in the end, and when the stalls flew open at Epsom he was 4–1 favourite. A measure of the bookies' fear of Piggott's ninth possible Derby triumph and the punters' great love for the record-breaking rider was the fact that minutes before the off his odds were trimmed from 13–2. It takes a mountain of money, like a vault at the Bank of England, to change odds so drastically just before the Derby.

There was, however, no fairy-tale ending for the Sangster, O'Brien, Piggott trio. Inkerman finished 21st behind Shirley Heights, who started Greville Starkey's fabulous season by beating Hawaiian Sound, for whom Sangster had enterprisingly flown legendary American rider Willie Shoemaker over. Would Lester have won on Hawaiian Sound? I have a hunch that he might have done. He would not have come off the rail and remembering the Roberto and The Minstrel finishes I think Piggott's immense power would have done the trick.

Shoemaker was then third on Hawaiian Sound in the Irish Derby, when Inkerman and Lester were fourth.

Hawaiian Sound's great moment came in the Benson and Hedges at York. This time Piggott was in the saddle. He attempted to make all and the combination of a horse with a heart full of courage and Lester's relentless driving accounted for a class-packed field. Did Lester learn from 'The Shoe' which were the best tactics? No way.

After the race the irony of winning on a horse on which his so-called American equal had been beaten was not lost on Piggott.

Sangster approached the 'Long Fella' after the race and said: 'I think I owe you a nice present. What would you like?' Back came the answer: 'What it cost you in air fares to fly that Shoemaker all the way over from America ... TWICE.'

In the racing calendar there remained only two big races which in his fabulous career Piggott had failed to win ... the early-season Lincoln Handicap and the Cambridgeshire Handicap at the back end. Yearly punters fling a fortune on Lester's intended rides in the Lincoln and Cambridgeshire in the hope that he will break his duck. Horses he picks to ride are all the rage in the ante-post betting. Horses linked with the 'Long Fella' are slashed in the odds. Were they to be ridden by any other jockey they would be 50–1 no-hopers. With the Piggott booking they become 8–1 favourites.

The power of Piggott in the million-pound betting industry was never more clearly demonstrated than in the autumn of 1978 when his name was linked, though not confirmed, to ride in the Cambridgeshire Jeremy Tree's Home Run, who had shown a bit of class the previous autumn when Lester had ridden him to be third behind Dactylographer and Julio Mariner in the William Hill Futurity.

Immediately Home Run was cut by the bookies from 33–1 down to 20–1, and two days before the race he was 6–1 favourite having been laid to lose a king's ransom. Maybe the Piggott Cambridgeshire jinx struck again for Tree rang his stables from Newmarket Sales on the Thursday only to learn that the colt had gone lame and was a non-runner.

This sparked another monster Piggott gamble when he agreed to ride Colonel Parker for Neville Callaghan. Within seconds his odds came tumbling down from 25–1 to 12–1. He started at 11–1 but was 13th.

Piggott seldom picks the wrong one but he did for the 1978 Champion Stakes. He teamed up with Hawaiian Sound again but it was the filly Swiss Maid, ridden by Starkey, who relegated him to second place. There was a great irony behind this shock result as Swiss Maid had always been reluctant to go into the stalls and Paul Kelleway spent hours at Newmarket in Piggott's own barn coaxing the filly in and out of stalls. Lester must have looked on with annoyance as Swiss Maid, for whom he was provisionally booked to ride, swept by him. Lester in fact gave up several hours to Swiss Maid, assisting Kelleway.

So the Cambridgeshire and Lincoln remain the two bogey races. An amusing story comes from little David Maitland, who has won two Cambridgeshires on Dites (1966) and Flying Nelly (1974). After Flying Nelly's win a beaming Maitland strode into the weighing-room. He recalls: 'I looked across at Lester and said, "Oh, well, that's two Cambridgeshires I've won. How many have you won, Lester?" The next second I was ducking as a boot came flying across the room.'

Piggott drew a complete Classic blank in 1978. Ile de Bourbon was backed like a certainty down to 11–8 on but continued the year of the bookies and was a well beaten sixth behind 28–1 Julio Mariner. Piggott, who had said 'Ile de Bourbon won't be beaten. All the rest are handicappers', was tenth on Arapahos.

Lester made a mistake about Ile de Bourbon, whose sire Nijinsky had won the Leger for him eight years previously. He was also wrong about Solinus, who was just beaten by Sexton Blake in the 1977 Champagne Stakes. Said Lester to O'Brien: 'He needs further than this seven furlongs.' For once the 'Long Fella' was proved wrong, and in 1978 Solinus, a fine looking colt, turned out to be Europe's outstanding sprinter. He won the King's Stand at Royal Ascot, the July Cup at Newmarket and the William Sprint Championship at York. O'Brien was forced to admit: 'He's the best sprinter I have ever trained.'

Choosing Lester Piggott's best ever single riding performance is like trying to select Sir Donald Bradman's greatest innings. Runs flowed from the latter's bat with just the same regularity as Piggott has pounced on his unfortunate rivals. How many jockeys over the years must have thought they had a race in the bag only for the 'Long Fella' to come along with a devastating run to steal victory from defeat?

Peter Scott, Hotspur of the *Daily Telegraph*, singles out the St Leger win on Ribero in 1968. Says Peter: 'It was an absolutely masterful example of nursing a horse home. Ribero was not an easy ride and definitely not a true stayer. The ground was also soft, so that was against his great finishing speed. Everything was against Ribero but Piggott nursed him to victory beautifully.'

Alleged is Christopher Poole's immediate selection. The *Evening Standard* correspondent told me: 'Despite a career of over thirty years as a master tactician, Piggott has never ridden a better race. Who else in the world would have dared set his own pace virtually from the start to perform that most difficult tactic of waiting in front? Then with his unique combination of strength and timing he went on to beat off one challenger after another in the seemingly endless Longchamp straight.'

Racing writer and historian Richard Onslow told me: 'Lester's best display for me was on Casabianca in the 1965 Royal Hunt Cup. Nobody else could have got him home. His power that day was breathtaking. Another wonderful ride was on Twilight Alley in the 1963 Ascot Gold Cup. The way he waited in front was remarkable. He led all the way and played with the opposition.' By the end of the 1978 season Piggott had, in fact, won ten Ascot Gold Cups – yet another remarkable feat by the wonder rider.

The popular John Oaksey singled out Lester's Derby win on Roberto, and added 'But I don't suppose Roberto would agree' – a reference to the fact that Piggott had to beat the horse hard in the closing stages to inch clear of Rheingold.

Brough Scott, for several years Piggott's 'ghost' on his column in the *Evening Standard*, selects two unexpected races as the pick of Lester's mercurial powers: 'His riding of Pollerton for Tom Jones in the Scandinavian Open in Copenhagen had to be seen to be believed. In the closing stages he jumped at the horse with the same machine-gun tactics which won the Derby on The Minstrel. Some ex-Arthur Budgett apprentice was up against him in the finish that day. I don't suppose he'll ever forget the way Piggott went past him.

'On a horse called Ramirez in the Grand Prix de Dieppe a few days later we saw the other side of Piggott's artistry. Here he eased the horse home very effectively with no suggestion of the whip. It was a lovely sunny afternoon and it was pure magic to see Lester do his job so beautifully.

'Ghosting the maestro was great fun. He always insisted on reading the final product. He'd go through like a sub-editor and would always point out if I had spelt a foreign horse or race incorrectly.'

I know of only one man in racing who continually looked down on Piggott – Alec March, for 25 years the Jockey Club's senior starter with a record 101 Classic starts to his credit. High up on his rostrum, before the advent of starting stalls, March watched like a hawk for jockeys trying to 'beat the gun'. Yet over the years he had a happy association with Lester. Now retired, Alec March recalls: 'I started Lester in the very first race he won at Haydock when he was only 14. He always rode with a beautiful long rein. You never saw him grabbing a horse by the ears.

'One of my best memories of him was at the start of the July course at Newmarket. The horse stood there without a care in the world, as did Piggott. It was a pleasure to watch a great horseman and his horse. It's a memory which will stay with me until I die.'

Lester's worst display? In recent years I would have to single out his riding of the sprinter Music Boy in the Tattersalls' Yorkshire Nursery at York on May 13, 1975. Music Boy had already flown in at Ripon and Catterick, but as the usual jockey Johnnie Seagrave was suspended Snowy Wainwright put up Piggott.

'Music Boy was an out-and-out sprinter,' recalls Snowy. 'I told Lester that he was to jump out and make all. If he was five lengths clear halfway he was still to kick on. Halfway he was cruising and had them all beat, but Lester didn't kick on and Royal Boy came and did us by 1½ lengths.

'I was furious and told him: "You'll never ride for me again." Harsh words were spoken but he replied: "He's been beaten by a good horse."' *Raceform* commented: 'Music Boy broke very fast and had his rivals in trouble two furlongs out, but instead of kicking further clear his rider sat still. When challenged inside the final furlong Piggott pulled out all the aids, but Music Boy had nothing more to offer. Had more use been made of him, he would have taken some beating.'

Says Wainwright: 'People said I was daft to tell Piggott how to ride. They said I was talking through my pocket. But I proved my point as Music Boy went on, ridden by Johnnie Seagrave, to win at Epsom, Ascot, and then the Gimcrack at York. I still think that Lester's the greatest. But he made one mistake – I make them every day.' Piggott has not ridden again for this trainer. Ace commentator Peter O'Sullevan recalls another occasion when Lester's performance gave cause for argument: 'One day in France Lester was told by a top owner: "This horse is a certainty – just launch him two furlongs out and you'll win by a minute."' Piggott was in fact always a furlong behind and told the irate owner afterwards: 'Sorry, guv'nor, I couldn't get the blighter off the launching pad.'

Lester's win on The Minstrel in the 1977 Derby was yet another display of his genius. No other jockey in the world but our hero would have urged Robert Sangster's colt over the line by a neck. He was riding in his 25th Derby, and long after his retirement racegoers will recall the finish he rode at Epsom that day. Just as he had relentlessly outgunned Ernie Johnson on Rheingold with Roberto in 1972 by a short head, so this time his driving finish left Royal jockey Willie Carson the luckless runner-up on Lord Leverhulme's Hot Grove by a neck. In recent years The Minstrel has been regarded as a very fitting winner for Piggott in his 25th Derby, and also in the Queen's Silver Jubilee year.

But in reality The Minstrel probably only ran in the Derby as a last resort on the part of the O'Brien, Sangster, Piggott team. The Minstrel, like so many Ballydoyle in-mates, was bred in the purple. Class oozed from his pedigree and if ever a horse was born to win a Derby, this was it. He was a flashy sort, which can arouse great fears in some breeding experts. He was an exceptionally bright chestnut with a bold white face and four very distinctive white socks. Like so many winter ante post favourites for the 2,000 Guineas and Derby, he had won the Dewhurst Stakes at Newmarket in the autumn. Now he was red-hot favourite for the Guineas, but he won few friends when he won his first three-year-old race, the Ascot 2,000 Guineas Trial. The race was run in desperate ground but he came off a straight line in the last furlong and this combined with his flashy looks caused many experts to think that he might not have been too genuine. He also blotted his copy-book by running with his head in a slightly ungainly fashion. The knockers started to knock. 'Flash Harry' got plenty of stick in the press.

He started 6–5 favourite for the 2,000 Guineas and was a giant disappointment. Piggott put him into the race at the Bushes but his challenge went out like a light . . . and with it thousands of ante post Guineas vouchers. The Canadian-bred colt did lose a few lengths at the start but he was no match for the winner, Nebbiolo, and Tachypous. It is claimed that the appropriate parties kept faith in The Minstrel, but there was little else they could do and he duly re-appeared in the Irish 2,000 Guineas. This time he went one better and finished second behind Pampapaul. He was an easy 7–4 favourite at the Curragh and became very stirred up by one of the other runners being plated. Two furlongs out Piggott put him into the lead but he was slightly interfered with by Nebbiolo. Nevertheless he had every chance, but he still went down by a neck. It was not often that Piggott lost a photo finish in a Classic – especially to the little Italian jockey Franco Dettori!

The Minstrel's career appeared to be on the slide. Beaten in both the English and Irish Guineas there seemed little hope of glory in the Derby. This is where the evidence changes. Robert Sangster always insists that as he was leaving the Curragh after the Irish Guineas Piggott said, 'Oh well, there's always the Derby. I'll keep faith in him and he'll go well at Epsom.' Other information from France suggests that the 'Long Fella' did his level best to get on the Aga Khan's red-hot Derby favourite Blushing Groom. Rumours were rife that Piggott would get on to Blushing Groom in place of Henri Samani, whose Epsom experience was limited to say the very least. But Piggott's pre-Derby powers of persuasion for once failed to do the trick and Samani duly appeared on the 9–4 favourite. Trained by the French veteran François Mathet, he had turned the 2,000 Guineas into a procession and trotted up by three lengths. There were doubts about him staying 1½ miles but it was generally agreed that with Piggott on top he could have been kidded round Epsom.

With no chance of getting on Blushing Groom, Piggott's attentions turned totally to The Minstrel. After the race Vincent O'Brien said, 'It was only Lester's faith that made me run the horse at all.' Perhaps the wizard of Tipperary didn't know of the pre-race discussions that went on. O'Brien was aware that The Minstrel had become very excited in his Guineas pre-parades. Unlike Michael Stoute, who in 1985 encouraged Piggott to canter off to the start of the Guineas on Shadeed, miss the parade, and incur a £550 fine, O'Brien had other ideas – simple but effective. He pushed a wad of cotton wool into the ears of The Minstrel so he could not hear Epsom's annual noisy hurly burly of 250,000 racegoers, bands, and loud speakers. It proved to be a typical master stroke. The Minstrel strolled round the preliminaries in a far more settled fashion. He didn't appear to have a worry in the world. He came down Tattenham Hill like a bird and contested the lead with Hot Grove from the three-furlong marker. From then on it was The Minstrel and Piggott closed in bitter battle with Willie Carson and Hot Grove. But Lester waved his famous wand to perfection and got up in the last few strides to win by a neck. Blushing Groom finished third, but it must be stated that his jockey Henri Samani did nothing wrong. 'King Lester the Eighth' ran the huge banner headline in *The Sun* the next day, and The Queen herself was there at Epsom to see the terrific ding-dong battle.

Talk of The Minstrel being a flashy disappointment was now all forgotten, and he further enhanced his reputation and his potential stud value with an easy 1½-length win in the Irish Derby. The only problem for Piggott this time was the agonizing 15 minutes afterwards when the stewards heard an objection by the runner-up, Lucky Sovereign's jockey Frankie Durr. Piggott hit the front 2½ furlongs out on the 11–10 favourite, and as he looked over his shoulder for any possible threat, The Minstrel started to drift a little towards the stands. Durr said: 'Technically I felt I had a decent chance of getting the race. My fellow was making his effort when Lester's horse hung left and it did not do my chance any good.' The stewards took a different view, however, and The Minstrel kept the race. He therefore joined the élite band of Santa Claus, Nijinsky and Grundy to pull off the Epsom–Curragh Derby double at that stage.

Cotton wool was again put in The Minstrel's ears before the start of his next race, the King George VI and Queen Elizabeth Diamond Stakes at Ascot. This trick seemed to work perfectly as he behaved exceptionally well before the start and in the parade. Piggott struck the front at the distance but Pat Eddery on Orange Bay gave him a tremendous battle all the way to the line. The combination of Piggott's power and The Minstrel's undoubted bravery won the day by a short head. The Minstrel had now emerged as a really top-class three-year-old and hardly seemed the same horse who had flopped in both the English and Irish Guineas.

By 1977 the Robert Sangster racing empire was really taking off. 'I went to Vincent O'Brien – the best judge in racing – and that's how it all started,' says the modest Vernons pools supremo. It was down to O'Brien's rare insight to realize the potential of the great American sire Northern Dancer, which really sparked off their glory years. The Minstrel was retired to stud after the King George VI and sadly his talents were never tested in the Arc. But Piggott duly won the race for the first of two times on Alleged. Piggott's position as first jockey to Sangster seemed as firm as concrete, although there were the occasional rumblings that Piggott's displays on the Ballydoyle gallops were not everything that O'Brien wished for. These were the days when horses started to be seen more as potential stallions than actual racehorses – a sad trend for punters and racegoers. Piggott was quoted as saying 'The best horse I have ever ridden' about Dewhurst winners Try My Best, Monteverdi and Storm Bird. This no doubt added millions to their stud value but they were hopeless flops as three-year-olds. Piggott struck a Classic blank in 1980 and there were signs that his partnership with O'Brien was about to crack up. Sure enough, despite several denials, it was officially announced that Pat Eddery would take over as first jockey at Ballydoyle. Piggott, who had split with Sir Noel Murless in 1967, was not pleased: when he first quit Warren Place to join O'Brien it had seemed something of a disaster, as the next year Murless picked up Classic wins with Royal Palace and Fleet in the hands of Australian George Moore.

But if anybody thought that Piggott without O'Brien and Sangster would be an idle jockey they could not have been more wrong . . . and the prodigal son was about to return once more to Warren Place.

CHAPTER NINETEEN

'I never knew they cared'

Virtually all of Lester Piggott's Classic triumphs have been surrounded by one kind of pre-race controversy or another. The great man seems to court controversy with alarming regularity. But his brilliant victory on Fairy Footsteps in the 1981 1,000 Guineas was probably the most amazing of all his Classic conquests. For exactly one week before he urged Henry Cecil's filly home at Newmarket by a neck, Piggott was involved in a horrific accident at Epsom and was extremely lucky not to lose his right ear completely. Many of Lester's big race wins are a testament to his supreme horsemanship, but with Fairy Footsteps the racing world gasped yet again at the 'Long Fella' for the courageous way he had climbed from his sick bed in hospital to capture the 1,000 Guineas. His Classic win number 24 was a little bit special.

Piggott's agony started just before the start of the 3.35 pm Ladbrokes Westmoreland Hotel Sprint Handicap due to be run over five furlongs. The afternoon at the twisty-turny Surrey track had started well for the maestro when he won the big race, the Princess Elizabeth Stakes, on Daniel Wildenstein's good filly Petroleuse. Not for the first time Piggott had used all his artistry to outfox arch rival Willie Carson on Applemint in a hectic, half-length finish. Piggott is the King of Epsom, but now he was to experience his most terrifying moment ever in the saddle at the very course where he has so often stamped his greatness.

Millions of TV viewers saw the horrifying accident. Lester was riding Winsor Boy for Bob Turnell, better known for his jump racing exploits. As soon as the five-year-old gelding went into the starting stalls he started to panic. He then wriggled out of the stalls and viewers heard Piggott cry out in pain as he crashed off the horse. The horse then squeezed through the three-foot gap under the stall gate and Piggott cannoned into the woodwork. As the horse bolted down the track, Piggott was plunged to the ground but bravely tried to get to his feet. But as shocked racegoers pinned their 'bins' on the scene Piggott rolled on the turf for several seconds before collapsing unconscious. First aid men then rushed to the scene, and it soon became clear that Piggott's head needed to be heavily bandaged.

Fellow jockey Brian Rouse said, 'Lester was very lucky – his ear was badly torn and part of it was hanging off. The horse was panic-stricken and went wild.' Winsor Boy careered down the course and jumped off the rail knocking down a spectator, Mrs Valerie Cane. Then the terrified horse collapsed and died. Piggott was rushed off to Epsom District Hospital, his head well bandaged. Later he was moved to the Queen Mary's Hospital at Roehampton in South London where plastic surgery was performed on his ear lobe. A doctor told waiting pressmen, 'His right ear lobe was partially torn off. I am sure that he will recover but it will take a little time.' Susan Piggott was soon at his bedside and revealed, 'Lester says that he will be all right.'

Punters who had backed Fairy Footsteps down to even money favourite for the 1,000 Guineas were now resigned to the fact that their money would not carry Piggott in the Classic. How on earth could a man who had part of his ear severed and needed thirty-one stitches possibly get back in the saddle within a week? Fairy Footsteps was evens to win but Piggott seemed 100–1 for making a dramatic come-back. As he recovered from being dragged at Epsom Piggott was swamped with letters and get well cards. He said, 'I never knew you cared quite so much. I never knew that there were so many people who cared about me. Lying there on the ground I honestly thought that it would possibly be the end of my career. I felt that my back had gone. The ear was in fact the least of my worries. Two things made me get back – the thought of riding Fairy Footsteps in the Guineas, I knew she'd win, and the hundreds of letters and cards I received from the public.' Lester's quote of 'I never knew they cared' is a classic. He should have known that millions of race fans and anybody who has ever had two bob on a nag would care desperately about the well-being of the genius. With the attraction of riding Fairy Footsteps in the Guineas, Lester would probably have defeated even more serious setbacks to get in the saddle. The thought of turning on the television to watch somebody else win on his big race ride would probably give him far more pain.

Having parted with Robert Sangster at the end of 1980, Piggott's career now returned to Warren Place, the magnificent mock-Tudor house and stables just outside Newmarket. Backed by Henry Cecil he seemed certain to become champion jockey for the tenth time. Lester pointed out that the last season he rode for Sir Noel Murless at Warren Place he had had his best ever season with 191 winners. The bookies were taking no chances and made Piggott odds-on to become champion again in 1981. Cecil's blue-bloods looked a very powerful unit.

As a two-year-old Jim Joel's filly Fairy Footsteps had been ridden by three different jockeys – Pat Eddery, Joe Mercer and Bruce Raymond. Cecil is unorthodox as a trainer in many respects, and is never frightened of letting loose the most exciting of his string at the most lowly of tracks. Yarmouth, Leicester and even little Folkestone have seen the début of some of his subsequent Classic heroes. Fairy Footsteps made her debut at Sandown in July 1980, and Mercer was on her as she finished a respectable fourth in the Raynes Park Maiden Stakes. Bruce Raymond took over the ride when she had her next outing in the Sweet Solera Stakes at Newmarket in August. This time she finished second to Michael Stoute's Exclusively Raised. There was no real indication that this was a Classic filly in the making. She was allowed to start at a generous 4–1 for her third and final race as a two-year-old. This time Pat Eddery took over the reins in the Waterford Candelabra Stakes at Goodwood in August. Piggott was on the favourite Exclusively Raised but it was a very different story from their recent Newmarket clash. Eddery made every yard of the running on Fairy Footsteps and slammed Madam Gay by four lengths. The horse also smashed the course record for fillies running over seven furlongs. So when Piggott returned as top pilot of the Warren Place set, Fairy Footsteps was one of several exciting inmates.

Cecil does not usually have any runners until the Craven meeting at Newmarket. Fairy Footsteps duly reappeared in the Ladbrokes Nell Gwyn Stakes on 16 April. Word had obviously got around among the touts at headquarters that the filly was moving well and she started 6–4 on. Piggott rode her with the utmost confidence. He obviously knew that he had a real champion under him. The attractive half-sister to Cecil's St Leger winner Light Cavalry turned in a pillar to post job and had 2½ lengths to spare from Shark Song at the finish. It was a most impressive Guineas trial and Fairy Footsteps was made the red-hot favourite for the big 'un. Not only was she bred to get further than a mile; she also possessed a great deal of speed. All seemed set for Cecil and Piggott to open their Classic account . . . until the Epsom crash.

While Piggott recovered at home from his plastic surgery, Cecil called up Pat Eddery to partner Home on the Range in Sandown's April Maiden Stakes on 24 April. The fact that Lester learnt that Eddery had got Louis Freedman's filly home by a neck probably made for an immediate improvement in the great man's health. The following day saw Shergar burst onto the Classic scene when Walter Swinburn galloped away from his rivals to win the Guardian Trial by an amazing ten lengths. Piggott no doubt watched the race on TV and noted the ease with which the Aga Khan's colt murdered his rivals. Yet again the cards were to be dealt in such a way that Lester didn't even miss out on the Shergar roundabout.

Cecil maintained that he hoped Lester would recover in time to ride Fairy Footsteps. Knowing Piggott's fantastic keenness to snatch Classic glory – and the huge financial rewards which go with it – we should have all known better. Exactly a week after that awful fall at Epsom, Piggott marched out to ride Victory House in the May Malden Stakes at Newmarket – the first race on the 1,000 Guineas card. It was clear that Lester was riding in a specially padded helmet. There was no fairytale return in the first race as Piggott finished third. Video Tape was made 9–4 favourite for the Heathorn Stakes but could only finish fifth behind the northern-trained Shotgun. Guy Reed's colt was another horse that Piggott was later to climb aboard surrounded by controversy.

But now the stage was set for Fairy Footsteps and Piggott's 24th Classic win. Later Henry Cecil revealed that he thought more of the filly as an Oaks candidate and the Guineas was just something of a bonus on the way. She was bred to get 1½ miles and seemed to have the ideal temperament for big races. I recall watching her striding around in the paddock before the Guineas. There was great excitement surrounding her – and particularly her jockey – but she took it all so calmly. Veteran owner Jim Joel had won every Classic apart from the Oaks. In Fairy Footsteps he was convinced that he could complete his Classic account. Joel was especially keen to win the Oaks as his West Side Story had been beaten by a short head in 1962.

There is no bigger leg-puller in racing than Greville Starkey. His Jack Russell dog impersonations have scared many an old lady and posh restaurant manager. He was riding Go Leasing, the eventual third in the Guineas, and drew the official starter's attention to an ear that was lying on the ground by the starting stall. Piggott produced a rare grin as he realized that Starkey was up to his tricks with this rubber look-alike ear.

Fairy Footsteps eased out from evens to 6–4. Perhaps the bookies imagined that Piggott was not 100% fit. They could not have been more wrong. There are so many aspects of

Piggott's genius in the saddle but none more significant than his ability to wait in front with a horse. He has a brilliant split-second ability to pace himself throughout a race, thus controlling the entire contest. This he did to perfection on Fairy Footsteps. Her main rival appeared to be Michael Stoute's Marwell. She was later to go for a sprinting career. Piggott knew that Fairy Footsteps had the one trump card – she would stay for ever. The ideal tactics were to stretch her rivals, and this he did to perfection. In the Dip it seemed that Edward Hide on Tolmi might upset the apple-cart but Piggott went for his whip and managed to hold on by a neck. Marwell finished fourth in a desperate finish. A length and a half covered the first six home but it was Piggott's flair which shone out that afternoon. As John Sharrett, the very experienced race-reader with Raceform, commented on Marwell, 'She met one holding all the aces.' Many punters no doubt thought that Piggott had done a reasonable job in getting home the favourite. Subsequent events may have proved that it was one of his greatest-ever rides, getting the filly to triumph by a neck. Looking back at the race with the benefit of hindsight, Fairy Footsteps was probably flat to the boards and needed every pound of Piggott's strength. And this from a man who a week before was lying concussed on the Epsom turf.

Fairy Footsteps was now virtually unbackable for the Oaks. She seemed to have the Epsom Classic at her mercy. But her reputation and her entire career were blown sky-high at York. She started 9–4 on for the Musidora Stakes but flopped badly into third place and was never seen on a racecourse again. Piggott seemed to be going well on her and when he went to the front three furlongs out he looked back for any possible dangers. There didn't seem to be any problems. But suddenly the alarm bells were ringing and she was well beaten by Irish-trained Condessa and Paul Kelleway's Madam Gay. Immediate impressions were that she might not after all have got the one mile, 2½ furlong trip.

At Newmarket it was rumoured that Fairy Footsteps had

not set the world alight after her Guineas victory. Her York defeat was never quite explained but she had obviously gone over the top and she never raced again. Jim Joel's Oaks jinx had struck again. But at least racegoers have the memory of Piggott climbing from his sick bed to come back to ride her to perfection in the Guineas. So often the roulette wheel of fate seems to come up with Piggott's number – so it was after Fairy Footsteps' dismal and very expensive exit. She missed the Epsom Oaks . . . but Lester won the race anyway on Blue Wind and just for good measure he also won the French Oaks on Madam Gay. Former jump jockey Paul Kelleway is often dubbed 'Pattern Race Paul' because of his sky-high optimism and tilts at the big races. Madam Gay had failed to win any of her four previous races before the French Oaks at Chantilly – and she didn't win any of her five races as a three-year-old afterwards. But Piggott won the French Classic for the second successive year on Madam Gay, just as he had triumphed the previous year on Ian Balding's Mrs Penny.

It's dangerous to criticize a trainer as successful as Henry Cecil. But it is a fact over the years that some of his Derby and Oaks hopes seem to fade out of the picture after the Guineas period. Fairy Footsteps was a classic example, and in 1981 there was no suitable Derby ride from Warren Place for Piggott to partner. So yet again the annual Piggott Derby ride guessing game was under way. His name was linked with half a dozen horses. Punters were left in the dark as they tried to guess which colt the great man would climb aboard at Epsom.

Piggott was involved in the Bill Williamson 'jockeying off' stakes on Roberto in 1972. That incident left a nasty taste in people's mouths. But then it must be remembered that Piggott had lifted Roberto home by a short head. Nobody can be sure that Williamson would have won that day.

In 1981 it was the turn of luckless northern jockey Jimmy Bleasdale to get the Piggott chop from his Derby hope. Lester's name was associated with several Derby hopes but on the Saturday before the big race Piggott told pressmen 'I ride that grey'. Those few words meant that he had agreed to partner Shotgun in the Derby. Some days prior to this Piggott had approached Shotgun's owner Guy Reed and kindly offered his services. Reed, one of the country's top owner-breeders, had wanted 24 hours to deliberate. Not for the first time an owner was left with the big decision. Could he really snub Piggott's offer considering his un-equalled record in the Derby? Or should he remain loyal to his stable jockey? Reed went for the Piggott option just as most owners would do in that position. Said Reed, 'Business comes first before sentiment. The Derby is a race apart and Lester Piggott is Lester Piggott.'

Shotgun was trained by Chris Thornton, who said, 'I would have preferred Bleasdale but I perfectly understand Mr Reed's position.' Bleasdale, hailed as a future champion jockey at one stage before his career started to mark time, said, 'Of course I'm disappointed by Mr Reed's decision. The money is not all that matters. Everybody looks forward to riding a horse like Shotgun in the Derby. The race stands out on its own and you only get the chance of riding a winner once in a lifetime.' Before the Piggott booking Shotgun was an unfancied 25–1 shot. With the Lester rumours the odds were clipped to 14–1. With the official booking Shotgun suddenly became 9–1 second favourite. And it was just another example of Piggott's Derby power that Shotgun started 7–1 second favourite behind the 11–10 on favourite Shergar. In truth everything was against Shotgun. No grey had won the Derby since Airborne in 1946, and more importantly no northern-trained horse had lifted the crown at Epsom since Pretender way back in 1869. There's been a few northern pretenders in the Epsom line-up since then but not one of them has had the class to stick his nose in front. Piggott had never ridden Shotgun before the Derby. Shotgun had finished second in the Dante to Beldale Flutter. He was 50–1 for the Derby after that race but Bleasdale insisted, 'He's no 50–1 shot.' Reed, a no-nonsense north countryman, saw it differently. He said, 'If the blighter can't win the Dante I can't see him winning the Derby.' Reed was right. Money poured on Piggott on Epsom Downs and throughout the country. He was the obvious each-way chance to topple the mighty Shergar. Piggott was sixth into the straight on Shotgun and then had to work away like a demon. Shotgun hardly looked the part at Epsom and stayed very one-paced to finish fourth. He ran three more times that season but never won and was an expensive loser in the Mecca Scottish Derby, when he started 11–10 favourite, but Edward Hide finished fourth of five behind Little Wolf.

Shergar was a fabulous winner of the 1981 Derby. The Aga Khan's colt completely outclassed his rivals and young Walter Swinburn came home unchallenged by ten lengths. The cheeky lad even dropped his hands in the closing stages and gave Shergar a slap down the neck. Punters who took the 11–10 on never had a moment's worry. The race was over in a few strides when Shergar swept his way to the front at the foot of Tattenham Corner. He was also trained to the second by Michael Stoute, fast making a reputation for himself at Newmarket as an expert trainer, hungry for success. Walter's father Wally was one-time champion jockey in Ireland. Now the family dreamt of a Classic double. Walter was odds-on to win the Derby on Shergar and his father was eagerly looking forward to riding Dermot Weld's filly Blue Wind in the Epsom Oaks. But yet again the figure of Lester Piggott was lurking in the wings and he was to take over the leading role on the Epsom stage. Wally Swinburn, a much-respected rider in his native Ireland, had been pipped by a short head on Blue Wind in the Irish 1,000 Guineas. But as stable jockey to ambitious Weld he obviously expected to be on the filly in the Oaks. Weld and Blue Wind's American owner Bertram Firestone had other ideas. With Fairy Footsteps out of the way and Piggott available they upset all hopes of a Swinburn family double by engaging the 'Long Fella' for Blue Wind. Weld had taken over his late father's big Curragh stables. He had trained hundreds of Flat and jump winners but had never actually scored a Classic goal. In Blue Wind he thought he had the goods and wanted the best rider available. Piggott's knowledge of unique Epsom was obviously vastly superior to Swinburn's and that's why likeable Wally joined the ever-growing list of Piggott 'jocked off' riders. Unlike the famous Roberto and Commanche Run cases, I think that Swinburn would have won on Blue Wind anyway. Usually Piggott comes with a last gasp challenge at Epsom. On Blue Wind he swept into the lead two furlongs out and trotted up by seven lengths with Madam Gay second. She didn't win quite as easily as Shergar but it was one of the most clear-cut Oaks wins this century. Luckless Swinburn snr. regained the ride in the Irish Oaks and happily landed odds of 6–4 on.

The Swinburns suffered another blow when Walter picked up a ban from Royal Ascot which meant that he had to miss the ride on super Shergar in the Irish Derby. Yes, you have guessed . . . along came Lester Piggott to ride Shergar at the Curragh. Piggott easily won his fifth Irish Derby on Shergar, who started at 3–1 on. History was to repeat itself in 1985 when Swinburn picked up a ban from Epsom which wrecked his chances of partnering the red-hot favourite Shadeed in the 2,000 Guineas. Once more it was lucky Lester who stepped in for the big race ride, and although having to work much harder than expected he held on by a head to beat Bairn, the colt he would have ridden but for the controversial switch.

Swinburn was back on Shergar in the 1981 King George VI and Queen Elizabeth Diamond Stakes . . . and was given a return favour by Piggott, who rode Light Cavalry. Shergar was taking on older horses for the first time and was given a really remarkable piece of assistance by Piggott, who is not renowned for helping fellow jockeys out of a jam. Turning into the straight Shergar looked anything but a 5–2 on hot-pot as Swinburn seemed to be boxed in behind Master Willie and Light Cavalry. In all my years watching Piggott in action I've never seen him coming off the rail to let a rival through on the inside, but that is exactly what he did and Swinburn was able to kick for home and finally win by four lengths. Madam Gay was the slightly unlucky runner-up. Walter should have bought Piggott a nice big box of cigars after this extraordinary act of kindness.

Piggott was clearly enjoying life as Warren Place jockey. Gone were the long trips to Ballydoyle to gallop Robert Sangster's horses with Vincent O'Brien. Now Henry Cecil had all the big guns for Piggott to fire right on his Newmarket door step. It's hard to imagine two personalities in racing more unalike than Piggott and Cecil. Piggott is always ice-cool and unflappable with a face as expressionless as stone. Cecil is twitchy, nervous and always pulling faces. As a trainer he is far removed from the image of people like his father-in-law Sir Noel Murless. A flamboyant dresser, Cecil never uses binoculars. Unlike placid Piggott, Cecil admits to being a worrier. He'd love to cut back his string one day but probably never will. His partnership with Piggott saw two experts linked together. How sad that once again a tinge of bitterness and controversy was to destroy their double act.

The Cecil–Piggott team were at their peak at the 1981 Royal Ascot meeting. Lester landed his 100th winner at the Royal meeting and went on to gain his tenth win in the Ascot Gold Cup on one of his favourite horses, Ardross. On the first day Piggott scored a Cecil double on Belmont Bay and Strigida. But it was a bad meeting for punters and 14 losing favourites bit the dust before Lester came to the rescue on Ardross, the 100–30 on favourite. The previous year Ardross had finished second in the Gold Cup to Cecil's Le Moss. Charles St George then bought Ardross and switched him to Cecil. It was an inspired buy. One wag had commented of Ardross's Irish career, 'Ian Botham should have ridden him. He was hit so much.' He was to become one of Lester's favourite horses. In 1969 Le Moss won the Ascot Gold Cup and was then brought back to 1½ miles to win the Arc de Triomphe. The same plan was mapped out for Ardross. Piggott was seen at his cheeky best on

Ardross and kept looking over his shoulder at Willie Carson, who was riding away furiously but to no avail on the runner-up Shoot A Line. Piggott then won the Chesham Stakes on Cajun to raise his century of Royal Ascot winners.

But yet again Piggott was to be the subject of controversy when he finished fourth on Popsi's Joy in the Queen's Vase. The stewards took the view that Piggott should have finished the race third on the 6–5 favourite and imposed a fine of £100.

Ardross had the misfortune to be drawn 24 out of 24 in the Arc de Triomphe and that virtually put an end to his chances. But he gained revenge over Arc winner Gold River when Piggott partnered him to win the French St Leger at Longchamp on 25 October. This was a magnificent afternoon for the Piggott clan, as Moorestyle, snapped up in the sales by Susan Piggott and trained by her brother Robert Armstrong won the Prix de la Fort ridden by Lester. These were happy days for Piggott.

Suddenly it was smiling Piggott. He seemed much more relaxed and was even known to crack the odd joke – something unheard of in his early years. As sponsors of a race at Kempton, a carpet firm offered the winning jockey either a free carpet or the actual cat used in their well-known TV advert. Lester duly won the race. 'Do you want the cat or a carpet?' he was asked. 'I'd rather have a monkey,' he cracked, using the racing parlance for £500. He was dining with Jeremy Tree one evening when the ample trainer said, 'I have just remembered that I have agreed to go to Eton School to speak to the boys. What do you think, Lester, should I tell them about my stable, how to train, or what?'. Quipped Piggott, 'I should tell 'em you've got 'flu.'

Piggott's craving for winners was still fierce but one noted a general air of happiness. Said Cecil, 'Lester is more relaxed than he has ever been at any stage of his career. Being based in Newmarket now means that life is much easier for him and it's reflected in his attitude. I couldn't ask for a more conscientious stable jockey. He knows all the horses and their form backwards. He's not nearly so serious as people try to make out. He's got a wicked sense of humour. I've never had to tell Lester how to ride. I just leave it all to him. I've found it best with him not to ask about a horse the second he gets off it. Wait until later that evening or the next day. Lester will give you his opinion . . . and it's not often wrong. Lester's success has never gone to his head. He hasn't changed a bit since he was a teenager. He's very wise. But you could not meet a more modest man.'

Classic history was made in 1982 . . . Lester Piggott missed his first Derby for 20 years. Henry Cecil's Simply Great – not a very well named colt – won the Mecca Dante at York in good style and was being hailed as a possible ninth Derby winner for Piggott. But not for the first time in his career Simply Great had to miss the big race line-up. This left Piggott on the prowl for a Derby ride. In this mood Lester usually manages to pick up the very best of rides available.

But in 1982 he drew a complete blank, although he did manage to get a ride in the race after – on Johnny Nobody! Lester's quest for a good Derby ride proved simply useless. In face he received three open snubs. 'No chance,' came the reply from Michael Albina, who ironically was then Lester's tenant at his Eve Lodge stables in Newmarket. Lester was obviously after the ride on 12–1 Silver Hawk, whom he had ridden before.

Fabulously wealthy Greek shipping magnate Stavros Niarchos was the next man to give Piggott the rare Derby thumbs down. When Simply Great was pulled out the Sunday before the Derby, Lester was keen to get on Niarchos's Persepolis, a live 5–1 chance trained in France. Lester had won on him twice that season, but the Greek decided to stay loyal to top French jockey Yves Saint-Martin. The third rebuff came from 14–1 Super Sunrise's trainer Gavin Hunter. He had in fact tried to get Lester but the maestro, trying to keep all his options open as usual, tried to stall for 24 hours. Hunter would have none of it and booked Edward Hide. 'I think it's fairest to all,' said Hunter.

So Piggott had to watch from the stands for the first time since 1962 as part of the ITV team as Golden Fleece and Pat Eddery combined to give Robert Sangster his second Derby triumph to follow that of Lester on The Minstrel. Piggott tipped Persepolis in his ghosted column in a national daily. Persepolis finished fourth. Lester, in fact, drew a classic blank in England in 1982, but he was on the mark when winning the French 1,000 Guineas on River Lady (trained in France by François Boutin) for Robert Sangster. He was still riding occasionally in the famous blue and green silks.

Piggott was smack in the middle of a whipping row after the Free Handicap at Newmarket in 1982. He was accused of hitting a rival horse on the head before he won a photo finish on Match Winner. The incident produced two memorable quotes for waiting pressmen. The other horse involved was Mummys Game, ridden by Tony Ives and trained locally by Bill O'Gorman. It was after Ives finished fourth that he accused Piggott of 'repeatedly hitting my horse's head with his whip in the final furlong'.

Piggott was cleared of all blame by the stewards' inquiry and said, 'It wasn't a question of me hitting the other horse. Its head kept hitting my whip!' Strange to say the Newmarket stewards went along with that curious theory. Henry Cecil stood by Piggott and said, 'Was Lester supposed to stop riding because Ives wanted to come through?' O'Gorman was seething with anger at the stewards' verdict. He felt that the bigger Newmarket stables had triumphed over his smaller set-up and came out of the inquiry with the lovely line, 'It's the same old story. Christians 0, Lions 7.'

Diesis and Dunbeath were good autumn winners for the Cecil–Piggott team. But both proved expensive flops as three-year-olds. Touching Wood, ridden by Paul Cook, won the '82 St Leger and opened the Classic account for the mighty Maktoum family, who were to have such a huge influence on racing in the 'eighties.

But '82 ended on a sad note for Piggott. 'Stoneface Cracks' read the big headline in *The Sun* the morning after the Arc de Triomphe. This was the case of Lester's lost Arc on his favourite horse, Ardross. I wrote, 'Old Stoneface, Lester Piggott, had to blink away tears after failing by a whisker to capture Europe's richest prize in Paris.

'Piggott produced a vintage power-packed finish on Ardross in the £168,000 Arc de Triomphe at Longchamp. But the gallant partnership failed by a head to peg back the flying French filly Akiyda and her heart-throb jockey Yves Saint-Martin. Even before the result of the photo was announced the normally poker-faced Piggott stared balefully through tears and traces of mud and told Ardross's owner Charles St George "I've lost it." St George told me, "I can't remember Lester so upset. Ardross will never run again." '

Over 10,000 English fans were cheering Ardross and Piggott to the line but they couldn't quite do it. It was a case of so near but so far. Lester had to blink away his bitter disappointment but a record ninth Derby win was just around the corner. But even the form book wizard would have been pushed to name the colt at the end of '82 who was to give him further Epsom glory because the unfancied two-year-old was still a maiden. However, the Teenoso fairytale was about to unfold.

CHAPTER TWENTY

The lost Arc

Anybody who imagined that Lester Piggott would ease gently into retirement was in for a giant-sized shock. Controversy seemed to surround almost every move he made. But as ever his performances in the saddle were brilliant. Rows with owners, trainers and the Jockey Club did nothing to halt his appetite for success. Being stable jockey to Henry Cecil was a big bonus in his everyday life-style. The nearness of Warren Place was a decided advantage. But the storm clouds, which never seem to be far away in Lester's life, were gathering overhead. The first rumblings of what proved to be his very last owner-jockey split occurred at Goodwood in July 1983. The champion jockey was banned for five days for his 'careless riding' of Vacarme. The 3–1 on favourite had been first past the post only to be disqualified and placed last. If Piggott thought that he would get any sympathy from controversial French owner Daniel Wildenstein he couldn't have been more wrong.

Seething with anger at the way Piggott cheekily squeezed through on the rails in the final furlong of the Richmond Stakes, Wildenstein stormed, 'If Lester had done that in France, he would have been thrown out for a year.' Wildenstein's son Alec was also furious and told me, 'Lester enjoys giving us owners heart attacks. He had 10 lengths in hand. So why didn't he come on the outside?' Piggott was obviously less than pleased with the ban – and the open way Wildenstein, rather than defend his tactics, seemed to indicate that he thought the ban should have been longer. The split was inevitable.

The partnership with Wildenstein was completely blown in September. Wildenstein, who paid Piggott a sizeable retainer via Henry Cecil, assumed that the maestro would ride his filly All Along in the Arc de Triomphe. The filly's trainer, Patrick Biacone, stated quite firmly that Piggott would have the ride. But Lester rocked the racing set by saying that he would ride Awaasif for Sheikh Mohammed. It was at this stage of his riding career that Piggott seemed keen to court the Arab owners – no doubt with a view to the day when he would become a trainer. Wildenstein, always a man to speak his mind, exploded. 'That man will never ride for me again,' he said – and he has always stuck to his guns. Piggott claimed at the time, 'It's all a mix up. I never agreed to ride All Along. It's all most unfortunate and I hope it all blows over.' Guy Wildenstein, another son of the Paris-based art dealer, said, 'Piggott has not acted like a gentleman. My father has decided that he will never ride for us again.' Wildenstein duly replaced Piggott with Joe Mercer on the Cecil-trained Vacarme in the Middle Park Stakes. Cecil said, 'Mr Wildenstein feels that Piggott has let him down by not riding All Along. I don't think that Lester has acted very diplomatically. We have had a funny season with horses like Vacarme and Simply Great and he was looking forward to Lester riding All Along in the Arc.' With Piggott banned from the Wildenstein horses, Cecil's Warren Place yard was virtually split in two. The irony of the situation was compounded when several top-line jockeys, including Joe Mercer, turned down the Arc ride on All Along before it finally fell to Walter Swinburn. How Piggott must have cursed as Awaasif trailed in at the back and All Along sprinted home by a length. In fairness to Piggott it must be said that when he made his decision the ground was ideal for Awaasif and it subsequently changed dramatically in favour of All Along.

All Along, who started at 17–1, went on to a brilliant autumn career, so Piggott really missed the boat. Even in his moment of triumph Wildenstein could not resist saying,

'Ask Piggott how he feels.' Piggott mumbled, 'We all make mistakes. Who hasn't?'

Lester reached another milestone in his career on 13 October 1983 when he rode in his 10,000th race in England. He failed to win on Westview but made it winner number 4201 when Salieri won the next. That meant a 22% win record for Piggott over his 35 year career – a very high scoring rate for a jockey.

By June 1984 the Cecil–Piggott partnership was on the rocks. Denials were rife but finally on the eve of the Derby Piggott announced that their three-year spell was over. 'If I can't ride any of the Wildenstein horses there's no point carrying on there,' he said. So in 1985 Piggott branched out again as a freelance. Piggott's riding of Adonijah in the Prix Ganay at Longchamp raised a few eyebrows, including those of Henry Cecil, who thought that he had given the horse far too much to do.

Teenoso duly gave Piggott his ninth Derby victory. As a two-year-old Teenoso had failed to win in three races. When he came out as a three-year-old at Haydock, he failed to win by a neck in a maiden race won by Welsh Idol, who never won another race in his life. It was hardly the sort of start from a Derby winning campaign but the ground was poor. Teenoso then sprinted up under Steve Cauthen at Newmarket and the popular American went on to win the Lingfield Derby trial. It was the annual Piggott guessing game for the Derby and he was buzzing everywhere to ride horses in trials. 'I thought that he might ride Tolomeo for Luca Cumani or possibly one for Vincent O'Brien,' recalls Geoffrey Wragg, who was having his first season as a trainer after taking over from his veteran father Harry Wragg. 'But he came and rode Teenoso in a gallop and that was that. Teenoso had great stamina and I remember at the top of the hill at Epsom turning to my wife and saying, "I've never been so confident of winning a race in my life."' Piggott rode Teenoso as though he were a superstar that day. He sent Teenoso past the pacemakers at the foot of Tattenham Corner and went on to beat Carlingford Castle easily by three lengths. In a year dominated by cold and wet weather there was no doubt that Teenoso was the master at Epsom, steered to perfection by another master. Says Wragg, 'I didn't take a second suit with me to Epsom as I thought that it would be bad luck. I remember going to Lester's flat in London and changing into a sweater of his for dinner, which came half way up my arm'. Teenoso rather let himself down when being beaten at the Curragh in the Irish Derby and later at York. But Wragg insists, 'I never would have let him run at the Curragh if I had walked the track. It was far too hard.'

Later, in 1984, Piggott rode a peach of a race on Teenoso to win the King George VI and Queen Elizabeth Stakes at Ascot, and so vindicated owner Eric Moller's brave decision to keep this fine-looking son of Youth, the French Derby winner, in training as a four-year-old. Says Wragg, 'The excitement of watching Piggott at his superb best in the King George was even greater than winning the Derby. This time we were taking on all-comers of all ages. His masterly riding that day was almost frightening.' The pacemakers in the race were left behind and Teenoso was forced into an early lead. But Piggott did not panic and decided to make his best way home. The way Piggott won, so doubling Teenoso's value, was a moment of pure magic. Sadly he never ran in the Arc. But he did go to France for the Grand Prix de Paris at Longchamp, although unfortunately Piggott was reduced to a bloody mess down at the start when Teenoso suddenly threw his head back. Wragg recalls a good tale. 'There was some confusion about which prize I received after the race and which one went to Eric Moller. In the taxi on the way back after he had won Moller asked Piggott, "Did they give you anything?" Lester mumbled, "Yes, I got the coup de grace!" Moller, not really hearing, said "Oh, good. I'm glad you got something."'

Harry Wragg was a great fan of Piggott. Says Geoffrey, 'My father always asked me, "Did you get Piggott to ride that horse for us?" Whenever I say "No", he always says,

"That's buggered that then if Piggott fancies another one." '

Piggott won his 27th Classic when he won the '84 Oaks on Circus Plume, the race selected by Peter O'Sullevan as Lester's finest ever display. This equalled Frank Buckle's Classic record. Naming a Piggott error in a Classic is like looking for a needle in a haystack but his riding of Circus Plume in the Irish Derby must be open to question. Circus Plume may not have been able to lay up with the early pace but was eighth into the straight. Princess Pati made virtually all the running and was able to pinch the race with Piggott finishing second.

Lester's record-breaking 28th Classic win on Commanche Run had all the usual juicy pre-race drama. Luca Cumani, a very likeable Italian who has settled so well into the Newmarket scene, very enterprisingly brought over American Darrel McHargue to be his stable jockey. Piggott escaped serious injury after a horrifying fall from a horse in a Yarmouth seller. He was dragged along and painfully bumped on the ground. But two weeks before the St Leger he was back in business. He also spent a great deal of time ringing up Commanche Run's owner Ivan Allan, who had been a long-time pal. 'I'll ride that Commanche Run. He'll win with me on top,' insisted Piggott. Allan was not keen to upset Cumani, who always stated, 'McHargue is my stable jockey and there is no question of anybody else taking over. I'm more than satisfied with Darrel.' The phone line between Newmarket and Singapore was really buzzing as the big race date became nearer. 'I'll win with Commanche Run,' promised Lester, and the popular owner replied, 'That's like music to my ears – you now ride him.' Not for the first time a trainer was put in a totally embarrassing situation. But Cumani took the situation well. Having stated that McHargue would definitely be in the saddle, it was that man again who got the leg up and the American was given the Bill Williamson treatment. Not surprisingly, McHargue packed his bags at the end of the season and went back to America.

Commanche Run duly gave Lester Piggott his record 28th Classic win. 'Thank you, Lester,' was Cumani's sole comment when the maestro returned in front of a joyous Doncaster crowd. To be honest I don't think poor McHargue would have won on Commanche Run. It needed all Piggott's power to drive the horse home by a neck from Steve Cauthen on Baynoun. The two horses were locked in a tremendous tussle but yet again Piggott got the verdict in the photograph. Judge Michael Hancock had decided most of Piggott's photo finishes. 'You always spot that famous backside in a Classic photo – or so it seems,' says Hancock.

If Cumani did not want Piggott's services in the 1984 St Leger he got the great man on his colt Bairn for the 1985 2,000 Guineas . . . only to lose him. Now freelancing, Piggott was expected to partner Ravi Tikkoo's Kala Dancer and Kashi Lagoon in the Guineas. In fact, Tikkoo told me, 'I have a gentleman's agreement with Piggott that he rides Kala Dancer in all his races.' It didn't quite turn out that way and Geoff Baxter was on Kala Dancer, who had missed much of his pre-race work through injury. Cumani spoke at the Mecca press lunch before the Guineas and produced the best impersonation of Piggott's unusual accent I've ever heard.

Piggott stayed in Australia and missed the start of the Flat season. He was involved in a spot of bother over a TV insult. Australian sports commentator Rex Mossop interviewed Piggott and was very disappointed with the outcome. Said Mossop, 'So far as I am concerned Piggott is unintelligible. I know that Lester does not ride with his mouth but as far as I am concerned I couldn't understand him.'

Getting the accent off to perfection Cumani said, 'I got this phone call from Lester saying, "I'm back". Oh yes, I said. Jolly good. Two weeks later I got another phone call: "I'm back. How about me coming to ride Bairn?" No. I don't want you messing up my gallops.' Piggott duly got on Bairn for the Greenham, only the second race of his life. He scored impressively and Piggott agreed to ride him in the Guineas. Walter Swinburn incurred the wrath of Epsom stewards and was likely to be banned in the subsequent Jockey Club inquiry. This put him out of contention for the ride on Shadeed, who had trotted up in the Craven and was the red hot Guineas favourite. Brough Scott interviewed Piggott at Epsom and asked, 'If Walter is banned, will you be on Shadeed?' Piggott wasn't in the mood for revealing his moves. He had spoken to Michael Stoute about Shadeed but fended off Brough by saying, 'Suspended? I don't know anything about that.' Swinburn was duly banned for 21 days and Piggott scored his 29th Classic win on Shadeed in the Guineas.

Yet again there was more drama as the highly excitable Shadeed ducked the pre-race parade and Piggott cantered him gently down to the start. You might have imagined that Piggott would incur a fine but it was Stoute who picked up the £550 fine. 'I might have done punters a favour,' claimed Stoute. Piggott needed all his coolness and power to get Shadeed by a head from Bairn, who was partnered in the end by Willie Carson. Lesser jockeys may have panicked on realizing that Shadeed was not showing the same blistering speed which saw him spreadeagle his Craven rivals. But once again the cards had been dealt in Piggott's favour.

He was also somewhat fortunate to emerge unscathed when Henry Cecil was fined £2,000 by the Jockey Club for arrangements for the jockey's retainer at Warren Place and extra payments. An ex-owner of Cecil decided to spill the beans about the letter sent to Cecil's owners. At the end of the letter it said, 'It would probably be best if you destroy this.'

When Lester switches to training it will be at Eve Lodge in Hamilton Road, Newmarket. His former chauffeur Mick Hinchcliffe started training there at one time but with no great success.

Ex-jockeys who switch to training seldom set the racing world alight. Former jump jockey Michael Dickinson is the obvious exception. But it would take a very brave man to predict that Lester Piggott will not make a success of his new career when he finally hangs up those famous boots.

One thing is a certainty . . . we've never seen a better jockey. And you can bet your life that you never will.

APPENDIX

Piggott's domestic riding record (Great Britain) 1948–84
compiled by Neal R. Wilkins

	Won	2nd	3rd	Unpl	Mounts	Pos
1948	1	2	0	21	24	—
1949	6	8	10	96	120	—
1950	52	45	39	268	404	11th
1951	51	36	40	305	432	13th
1952	79	47	70	424	620	5th
1953	41	32	45	323	441	15th
1954	42	38	30	152	262	18th
1955	103	84	77	266	530	3rd
1956	129	79	75	359	642	3rd
1957	122	92	83	280	577	3rd
1958	83	81	64	309	537	6th
1959	142	96	85	236	559	3rd
1960	170	107	75	288	640	1st*
1961	164	108	73	358	703	2nd
1962	96	77	50	235	458	4th
1963	175	109	71	302	657	2nd
1964	140	106	70	310	626	1st*
1965	160	110	81	304	655	1st*
1966	191	89	101	301	682	1st*
1967	117	100	64	276	557	1st*
1968	139	98	75	268	580	1st*
1969	163	95	87	255	600	1st*
1970	162	110	68	246	586	1st*
1971	162	120	89	259	630	1st*
1972	103	69	74	218	464	4th
1973	129	80	58	216	483	2nd
1974	143	91	73	279	586	2nd
1975	113	88	61	265	527	3rd
1976	87	68	51	196	402	7th
1977	103	82	62	265	512	4th
1978	97	78	61	249	485	5th
1979	77	54	40	232	403	6th
1980	156	96	65	318	635	2nd
1981	179	113	87	324	703	1st*
1982	188	87	94	329	698	1st*
1983	150	109	64	318	641	2nd
1984	100	79	72	240	491	3rd
Totals	4315	2963	2384	9890	19552	

*11 times Champion Jockey   6 times third
6 times Runner-up   3 times fourth

Up to and including 2 October 1984

Piggott also rode in 56 hurdle races, winning 20 times

Index

215

220

221